write here write now

Orders: please contact Bookpoint Ltd, 130 Milton Park, Abingdon, Oxon
OX14 4SB. Telephone: (44) 01235 827720. Fax: (44) 01235 400454. Lines
are open from 9.00–6.00, Monday to Saturday, with a 24 hour message
answering service. You can also order through our website
www.madaboutbooks.com.

British Library Cataloguing in Publication Data
A catalogue record for this title is available from the British Library

ISBN 0 340 814632

First Published 2003
Impression number   10 9 8 7 6 5 4 3 2 1
Year   2007 2006 2005 2004 2003

Typeset by Fakenham Photosetting Limited, Fakenham, Norfolk.
Printed in Great Britain for Hodder & Stoughton Educational, a division of
Hodder Headline Ltd, 338 Euston Road, London NW1 3BH by Cox &
Wyman.

National Blind Children's Society: Charity Registration No. 1051607

write here write now

A collection of children's writing
from the 2003 awards.

Hodder & Stoughton

A MEMBER OF THE HODDER HEADLINE GROUP

CONTENTS

FOREWORD

Stephen Twigg, MP
Parliamentary Under Secretary of
State for Schools

The Write Here, Write Now writing awards support the National Primary Strategy, which combines excellence in teaching with enjoyment of learning. The Primary Strategy is building on the outstanding success of the National Literacy Strategy in improving standards of reading and writing in primary schools. But it also encourages children to be creative by equipping them with the relevant skills, and engaging them in learning that develops and stretches them and excites their imagination.

Write Here, Write Now 2003 achieved a record number of entries, over 34,000. I would like to thank Gillian Cross, Brian Patten, Adam Hart-Davis and Lizo Mzimba whose opening lines and advice provided the children with a powerful starting point for their writing. It was inspiring to see how the children used their imagination to develop such interesting and sometimes humorous pieces of work.

I would also like to thank everyone who contributed to the success of the awards this year, particularly the teachers for their continued support and the children who worked hard on their entries. It is encouraging to see that so many children are using a range of skills in their writing. I would like to thank the judges who read so many entries. They were looking for work of high quality that was creative, original and held the reader's interest.

We want learning in our primary schools to be vivid and real and an enjoyable and challenging experience. The Write Here, Write Now awards have given an excellent and stimulating opportunity to the children who took part and I hope they enjoyed writing their entries.

I hope you enjoy reading this collection of children's writing.

INTRODUCTION

The Write Here, Write Now writing awards demonstrate how many talented writers there are in Years 4 and 5 (ages 8–10) around the country.

There were four categories for children to choose from – Story, Poem, Persuasive Writing and, for group entries, Journalism. The Story category asked children to continue a story about a mysterious box left on a doorstep, written by children's author **Gillian Cross**. In the Poem category, they used lines from **Brian Patten's** poem about Winter as a starting point; while broadcaster and writer **Adam Hart-Davis** introduced the Persuasive Writing category by asking children whether it was better to be a child now or in Victorian times. Groups entering the Journalism category wrote a TV or newspaper report following advice from BBC *Newsround*'s **Lizo Mzimba** and a picture to get them started.

The regional and national winners are all published in this book, showing the high quality of the entries and the wide range of topics the children wrote about. The five national winners were chosen by a panel of well-known writers and experts after much deliberation. There are also Improvement Awards winners, written by children who were nominated by their teachers for making significant progress in their writing.

Sometimes funny, sometimes sad, but always entertaining, this collection demonstrates the depth of writing talent that exists among young people around the country.

The children's work has been edited only lightly to allow their individual voices and styles to shine through, and their ages were correct at the time of writing their entries.

 POEM

Brian Patten wrote...

Winter

Ambushing snowdrops, beheading buds,
Drowning daisies in sudden floods,

It looks like winter won't let go,
Arthritic fingers dipped in snow.

Grey mist clinging like old news,
Mr Brock taking one more snooze...

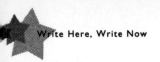

INTRODUCING THE POEMS

Brian Patten's atmospheric introduction was the trigger for a range of wonderfully creative poems. Many of the winning pieces concentrate on Winter, vividly exploring the sights and sounds of the season. But others explore a different angle – the change of the seasons through the year, or how different hemispheres experience different climates.

Georgina Izzard's poem powerfully conveys images of bleak winter weather, dark skies and icy temperatures. It makes you want to put on something warm as you read it! The fun aspect of Winter, and the excitement of skating, sledging and playing in the snow, is conjured up by **Alastair Horne's** piece. But, although he enjoys Winter, the return of the warm sunshine of Spring is something he looks forward to.

Charlotte Clarke's poem has a personal feel and follows on well from Alistair's. Having enjoyed the cold of Winter, Charlotte is tucked up warmly in bed looking forward to the prospect of Spring. **Jennifer Rowland** wonders when Spring will come, when the sun will wake up and the snowflakes be replaced by butterflies on the wing. Her evocative words convey a real sense of longing for the warmer weather to return.

Natalie Pearson's poem portrays Winter as an almost magical season – her descriptive words allow you to imagine the landscape, frozen in time, before Spring arrives. In his poem, **Joe May** captures the wider picture – icebergs drifting menacingly out to sea, a hazard for ships as they ghost through the water.

Hannah Roberts' poem likens the coming of Spring to a young puppy – a happy and joyful event. However, the mood becomes more sombre when the puppy goes out of the house and into the cold.

Jocelyn Murdoch explores the theme of warm weather returning after the snow and cold of Winter, and powerfully conveys the beauty and hope of a new Spring morning. **Amy's** expressive poem describes a snow-clad Winter, where trees and houses are hidden beneath a white carpet, but there is fun to be had by skating on the ice!

Charles Brice gives a very descriptive view of the season, and shows how Winter has its good points as well as its bad points – rosy cheeks but people coughing, warming stews but black ice, steaming cocoa but frozen locks.

A unique perspective is given by **Amy Knight** when she compares seasons in two different hemispheres. The picture of a cold, wintry England preparing for the Christmas season is neatly contrasted with a warmer climate, where barbecues, surfing and sandcastles are the order of the day.

Simon Monk-Chipman's poem is a tribute to the four seasons, giving each its own personality and suggesting an on-going battle as the cycle of the year unfolds.

Wicked Winter Worries

Ambushing snowdrops, beheading buds,
Drowning daisies in sudden floods,

It looks like winter won't let go,
Arthritic fingers dipped in snow.

Grey mist clinging like old news,
Mr Brock taking one more snooze...

A gloomy sky covering the land,
Dead trees alone they stand.

A swooping owl hoots in the night,
The whole landscape is covered in white.

Winter has come it won't go away,
What happens if it decides to stay?

Frost bitten faces, freezing fingers,
Grey skies and a mist that lingers.

Rusty cars with wind-whipped faces,
Sit alone in empty places.

Grey slush covers the icy road,
Lorries skid with their heavy load.

Misted up windows hunched together,
Animals can't bear this freezing weather.

Frost sweeps by like a battered broom,
Winter, why did you come so soon?

By Georgina Izzard, aged 10
Furneux Pelham C of E School

EAST OF ENGLAND WINNER

WINTER

Ambushing snowdrops, beheading buds,
Drowning daisies in sudden floods,

It looks like winter won't let go,
Arthritic fingers dipped in snow.

Grey mist clinging like old news,
Mr Brock taking one more snooze...

Flowers die now winter's arrived
Only evergreens have survived,

Swans sliding on slippery ice
Hot steamed pudding served by the slice,

Boys skating on icy puddles
Keeping warm in cosy huddles,

Dogs playing in deep drifts of snow
Cats lying by the fire's warm glow,

Dragging the sledge up the big hill
Zooming down is such a great thrill,

Warm sunshine and a gentle breeze,
Brings the end of the winter's freeze.

By Alastair Horne, aged 10
Cropthorne with Charlton CE First School

WEST MIDLANDS WINNER

Winter

Ambushing snowdrops, beheading buds,
Drowning daisies in sudden floods,

It looks like winter won't let go,
Arthritic fingers dipped in snow.

Grey mist clinging like old news,
Mr Brock taking one more snooze.

Outside covered with a blanket of snow,
Me in my bed wrapped head to toe.

Every tree bare to the root,
Like a skeletal hand, blackened with soot.

Icicles are melting drip by drip,
Trying their best not to loose their grip.

Winter is slowly fading away,
Its death is the start of Spring's birthday.

By Charlotte Clarke, aged 9
Threshfield Primary School

YORKSHIRE AND HUMBERSIDE WINNER

Winter Is Dying

Ambushing snowdrops, beheading buds,
Drowning daisies in sudden floods,

It looks like winter won't let go,
Arthritic fingers dipped in snow.

Grey mist clinging like old news,
Mr Brock taking one more snooze...

When shall the resting sun awake?
Butterflies and flutterbies instead of snowflakes,

When shall the seething wind begin sleeping?
The dark clouds flee and the sky stop weeping,

When will sombre Winter leave?
Along with the diseased, skeleton trees,

I have seen Winter fade like the damp morning dew,
Come and go, at birth and death,
I have seen Winter from one thousand different faces,
One thousand different pairs of eyes,

And yet again, the wind has stopped sighing,
Not for the first time, nor last, Winter is dying.

By Jennifer Rowland, aged 10
Hexham Middle School

  NORTH EAST WINNER

10

The Fourth Season

Ambushing snowdrops, beheading buds,
Drowning daisies in sudden floods,

It looks like winter won't let go,
Arthritic fingers dipped in snow.

Grey mist clinging like old news,
Mr Brock taking one more snooze...

Boughs heaped with soft white powder,
The wind can't howl any louder,

A blanket covers all that was alive,
But in spring again it will thrive.

Like a winter butterfly a snowflake flutters down,
to give the earth another silver crown.

Ice coats the lakes like the crust of apple pie,
While underneath fish do not cease to swim by.

Winter may seem like it will never leave,
But it is amazing what spring can achieve.

By Natalie Pearson, aged 10
Flora Gardens Primary School

LONDON WINNER

Winter Storms

Ambushing snowdrops, beheading buds,
Drowning daisies in sudden floods,
It looks like winter won't let go,
Arthritic fingers dipped in snow.
Grey mist clinging like old news,
Mr Brock taking one more snooze.

Silver-grey hairs floating,
Drifting to the paling floor.
Great sheets of ice cover the ground.
Gale forces attack with winter, blowing
Icicles, stalactites suspended from trees,
Out towards the sea.

Past the shore, past the ships,
Icebergs are huge silent monsters
Ghosting through the oceans,
A lethal hazard of icy waters.

By Joe May, aged 9
St Winefride's Catholic Primary School

 NORTH WEST WINNER

A season for a puppy

Ambushing snowdrops, beheading buds,
Drowning daisies in sudden floods,
It looks like winter won't let go,
Arthritic fingers dipped in snow.
Grey mist clinging like old news,
Mr Brock taking one more snooze
Before the spring arrives.

It comes like a little puppy
Running through the grass
Playing with his chew toy,
Jumping up at everyone he sees.
Looking up at the rose so dark,
The sunflower, yellow and tall,
The cloud-free sky –
The puppy's eyes light up
As he sees all these things.

Then suddenly
The sky goes grey
Everyone runs in the house
Leaving him all alone
In the garden barking away.
But no one listens to the puppy,
To what he is saying.
Everyone's inside watching TV
While the little puppy is scratching on the door.
But no one can hear him,
Sitting in the rain
While all the leaves are blowing off the trees.

By Hannah Roberts, aged 10
St Winefride's Catholic Primary School

AWARDS FOR IMPROVEMENT JOINT WINNER

Winter's End

Ambushing snowdrops, beheading buds,
Drowning daisies in sudden floods.

It looks like winter won't let go,
Arthritic fingers dipped in snow.

Grey mist clinging like old news,
Mr Brock taking one more snooze.

Locked in winter's cold heart sleep,
Icy ponds glisten under their sheet.

Breath like smoke in the cold,
As the white snow falls on the wold.

No sign of spring under his chill,
Everything standing icy and still.

Crescent moon's replaced the dead sun,
In this life, summer's long time gone.

Sun breaking in the misty dawn,
The start of a beautiful spring morn.

Warm air smells like sweet mown hay,
As blooms a new spring day.

No sign of winter under her sun,
All standing colourful and as one.

By Jocelyn Murdoch, aged 9
Sibsey Free School

EAST MIDLANDS WINNER

14

Winter's Here

Ambushing snowdrops, beheading buds,
Drowning daisies in sudden floods,

It looks like winter won't let go,
Arthritic fingers dipped in snow.

Grey mist clinging like old news,
Mr Brock taking one more snooze.

The snow is falling, white silent on the ground
When people walk over it you don't hear a sound.

Bare trees with no leaves, branches reach to the sky
A jumping dog lands in the snow with a cry.

Where is the green grass? It is covered white
Under the snow it is dark as night.

A sliding boy thinks it's so much fun to play on ice
Gliding along left and right, he does this twice.

Feet crunchy and crispy in the snowy lane
Snow falls from the squeaky gate when people open it late.

All houses will be covered in snow
Trees bending heavily, bending low.

When will winter end – I don't know
Spring is around the corner – hurry winter just go!

By Amy, aged 8
Bailey Green Primary School

AWARDS FOR IMPROVEMENT JOINT WINNER

Winter

Ambushing snowdrops, beheading buds,
Drowning daisies in sudden floods,

It looks like winter won't let go,
Arthritic fingers dipped in snow.

Grey mist clinging like old news,
Mr Brock taking one more snooze...

Rosy cheeks and chilblained toes,
Drips that trickle from your nose,

Fingers stiffened with the cold,
Extra heating for the old,

People coughing, sneezing too,
Winter colds and sometimes flu,

Hearty soups and warming stews,
Black ice mentioned on the news,

Misty breath, like smoking fags,
Extra blankets, sleeping bags,

Children wrapped in layers of clothes,
All you see is eyes and nose,

Snowman standing up our street,
Heavy skies and muffled feet,

Schoolboys slide and teachers fuss,
Snowballs pelted at the bus,

Car locks frozen, doors stuck fast,
Praying for the snow to last,

Puddles like glass which I stamp,
Pull the curtains, light the lamps,

Steaming cocoa late at night,
All outside is cloaked in white,

Robin's footprints in the snow
Where do homeless people go?

Bring on Winter, shut the school,
Snow's outside, I've lots to do.

By Charles Brice, aged 10
Wells Cathedral Junior School

SOUTH WEST WINNER
NATIONAL WINNER

17

The Hemispheres

Ambushing snowdrops, beheading buds,
Drowning daisies in sudden floods,

It looks like winter won't let go,
Arthritic fingers dipped in snow.

Grey mist clinging like old news,
Mr Brock taking one more snooze...

Across the world it's a different picture,
Barbecues on the beach with a spicy mixture.

People boogying with not a care in the world,
But in England, decorations are twirled,

Snow flakes different in every way,
Babies born and sleep and lay,

People preparing for Christmas Eve,
Sewing, knitting and colourful weave.

People surfing in the warm sea,
Balancing on a board, joining me,

While this hemisphere is wearing sandals,
England is cold and lighting candles,

Going off to sleep with a peaceful dream,
Christmas trees sparkle with a bright green.

The blazing fire, sausages, bacon and fins,
This helps people relax and drown their sins.

Gloves, mittens and scarves,
Throwing snowballs and loud laughs,

The sea's waves crashing loudly,
After this people sleep soundly,

People building high sand castles,
Children opening colourful parcels,

The sun heats the hemisphere sizzling hot,
While the carrots simmer in a pot.

The dinner is served with gravy and sauce,
Eating it with humour, munching each course.

To end this poem I'd like to say,
The hemispheres are different in every way.

By Amy Knight, aged 10
Southwater Junior School

 SOUTH EAST WINNER

19

Season Battles

Ambushing snowdrops, beheading buds,
Drowning daisies in sudden floods,
It looks like winter won't let go,
Arthritic fingers dipped in snow.
Grey mist clinging like old news,
Mr Brock takes one more snooze.

Along comes SPRING, lovely lady,
Come to fight old winter (lazy),
With her army of blossom,
And animals like the bird and possum.
Winter has his icicles,
But with spring's power, winter falls.

But soon SUMMER comes along,
And puts a stop to spring's song,
Here we go, another war,
Summer gets spring on the floor,
Summer's intense heat,
Looks like spring's dead meat.

A long while later here comes AUTUMN,
Taking on summer, yes he fought him,
He comes around like a tornado,
Calls the rain, ebb, and flow,
Autumn blows summer away,
Everyone cheers hooray.

By Simon Monk-Chipman, aged 9
Teagues Bridge Primary School

 AWARDS FOR IMPROVEMENT JOINT WINNER

20

PERSUASIVE WRITING

Adam Hart-Davis wrote...

Then or now?

Living in Victorian times, 150 years ago, must have been different in all sorts of ways from living today.

Children often had seven or eight brothers and sisters, and shared a bed with three or four of them. This may have been a bit crowded, but it was warm, and there was always someone to chat to.

They had one bath a week – in a metal tub in front of the fire downstairs. There was no toilet in the house, but there was a family privy in a smelly hut in the back yard. It must have been a bit scary going out there in the dark.

Today, children enjoy clever computer games and television. Victorian children made their own games, like skipping and hopscotch, but at least they didn't have to worry about power cuts or computer viruses. They could also play in the street, since cars hadn't been invented.

So, is it better to be living now, or was it better 150 years ago?

INTRODUCING THE PERSUASIVE WRITING

Have you ever wondered what it was like living 150 years ago in Victorian times? Can you imagine life without all the comforts we take so much for granted? In his opening piece, **Adam Hart-Davis** encourages us to think about how life would have been different back then – and what is better, and worse, about our lives today.

Nearly all of the winners in this section feel strongly that it is much better to be living today, rather than in Victorian times – and they argue their case quite strongly!

Lewis Bell comes down firmly in favour of modern life, arguing his case briefly but strongly, with lots of persuasive detail. He summarises by saying that children today have 'much better clothes, a healthier lifestyle and fantastic food!'.

'Going to the loo at night in a cobwebby hut' is one of the reasons **Kathryn Thompson** would not have been happy living in Victorian times. She uses an articulate and balanced argument, describing the modern aspects of life she would miss, not forgetting her mum's microwave and the family TV!

Lauren Coles also believes that life for children is better nowadays. Her voice comes through loud and clear as she explores how living conditions, education, entertainment and health would have been different in Victorian times.

24

The chatty, humorous style of **Hana Osborne's** piece really helps the reader to imagine life in Victorian times. Her descriptions of the schools, food and hospitals make you appreciate twenty-first century comforts! **Joanne Woodhams** also explores some varied aspects of Victorian life, and her persuasive arguments make it hard to disagree with her closing sentence.

Nicola Hinde's piece argues that 'children in Victorian times weren't really children'. Her very personal account explores the reality of living 150 years ago, as well as imagining the differences between the rich and poor.

Aisling Culhane takes a completely different approach, and argues strongly that children were less restricted in Victorian times. Her persuasive language clearly conveys the enjoyable, fun and adventurous aspects of being a child 150 years ago.

In contrast, there is no doubt that **Harry Riddle** would prefer to be a child today. There is a wealth of humorous detail in his account, which leaves you with a none too favourable impression of life 150 years ago! **Jade Healey** agrees with that point of view, painting a vivid picture of the harsh working conditions of Victorian England and appreciating the comforts of modern life.

Now or Then

Was it really so great in Victorian times? Think about it, there were an awful lot of fatal diseases and life was extremely dirty. I strongly believe that today's children live much better lives than a Victorian child.

An example of this is in Victorian times there were hundreds of deadly diseases which spread extremely quickly. Smallpox was a disease which was like measles. Tuberculosis was another big killer in Victorian times. It was a lung disease. In our day we've had vaccinations which have wiped out smallpox completely. We have superb scientists who are constantly coming up with new vaccinations to wipe out diseases.

In addition, in our day we have a lot more choice of food than in the Victorian era. Children today have a much wider range of food. We have microwave meals and oven meals. In the Victorian era children in the workhouse were given a liquid meal of water and oatmeal called gruel. I also believe that we have much healthier food than the Victorians. The food in the Victorian era was abysmal. We have fantastic food.

To prove my point children from the age of seven had to work down the mines. Was this good for them? They would be breathing the dusty dirty air and maybe even gas! This definitely wouldn't be good for them. How would you feel if your child went working down the mine at the age of seven? Today seven year olds go to school to learn and play, which they should be doing.

My conclusion is no matter what anybody says I believe today's child is much better off than a Victorian. We have much better clothes, a healthier lifestyle and fantastic food!

By Lewis Bell, aged 10
Mill Hill Primary School

NORTH EAST WINNER

Then or Now?

Many people would agree that the Victorian era would have been an intriguing time to live in, as they witnessed many important discoveries. Not me! I believe that our present time, 2003, is a better place for children to grow up in. For we have better hygiene and proper medicines, many of which can cure diseases which then were fatal.

The Victorians had poor toilet facilities which consisted of a small outdoor hut and a ditch dug into the ground. Every week or so a new ditch would have to be dug and the hut moved over it. Just imagine going to the loo at night, in a cobwebby hut, freezing cold and surrounded by bugs and insects. It was not hygienic.

Today, most of our household luxuries are powered by electricity. We take these things for granted and don't realise just how important they are. Of course the Victorians did not have electricity, can you imagine life without it? I know my Mum would miss her washing machine, my brother and I would miss TV and all my family would miss lighting. Just imagine, no playing after dark, going to bed early, getting around by candlelight and no heating. We are lucky.

Today we are fortunate enough to have a wide range of supermarkets to go to, which are always filled with a plentiful supply of foods. Nowadays we can just jump in the car and go to one of these supermarkets, whereas in Victorian times it was hard to get good food, and the food you did get was very little.

Furthermore, our education standards are far better now than they were then. For one thing you had to leave school four years earlier. I am a strong believer that, a child's education plays a big part in their later lives. Plus, the equipment then was very poor. The teachers were incredibly strict, as were the punishments for the slightest wrong doing.

To summarise, I think it is only right that children should grow up NOW because we have advanced medicines, superior education and a better way of life.

By Kathyrn Thompson, aged 10
Mary Exton JMI School

  EAST OF ENGLAND WINNER

Then or now

We all know what life is like now, busy but mostly happy. But 150 years ago life was different. Poor children had no proper education and started hard, dangerous work, many at the age of six. Houses were small and life was hard work. I believe that, for children, life is a lot better now.

Firstly, families then were poor and people often had six or more children. Most people lived in small crowded houses. Nowadays we live in comparatively big houses and most people have a fair amount of money. Then, four or five children shared a bed. I mean, would you want three or four people sleeping with you? What if one snored or wet the bed, or even had a contagious illness? There were no inside toilets then although there was a privy outside. Would you really want to have to go outside where it was often cold and dark at night to a smelly, dirty toilet? People only had one bath per week and must have smelt horrendous! There was no electricity either. Electricity is one of the things that make our lives much more comfortable. Clothes in those days were passed down from the oldest child to the youngest child. Just think of the state of the clothes by the time they'd got to the youngest! We're buying new clothes all of the time. In addition, only the rich children had education. Poor children worked! In the schools there were hard punishments for example, the cane. Children learnt the 3 Rs – reading, 'riting and 'rithmetic. The children were also taught the Christian religion.

Secondly, entertainment was totally different then. I suppose there was no need to worry about power cuts but children just played board games, ball games, skipping, hoop and stick and spinning top. They would probably get bored. Children could play in the streets. I suppose it was safer then as there were no cars. However, we've got computers, PlayStations, televisions, CD players and much more. So I think that we have more to do and we have more fun. In those days, families would sit and talk together as a pastime, but we have sports and activities and games as pastimes.

Furthermore, health 150 years ago was not good. For a start you had to pay to see the doctor and we all know how horrible it is to be ill and you want to get better immediately but the poor Victorian children could often not afford to be cured. Most had a limited diet as there was not enough money for a variety of foods. Poverty stricken families often sent their children to work, sometimes from the age of six, often as a chimney sweep or a miner or someone who worked in a factory with dangerous machinery. Some of this often led to death because of the smoke and acrid fumes in the air and machinery. If death did not occur then the children were often badly deformed. This isn't what a poor child deserves. Illnesses were also very common. Today this would not happen as there are strict rules about the employment of children.

I feel Victorian children were treated badly with no respect and little money and food. I believe that things should have been shared more equally. I feel that life now is most certainly a lot better for a child.

By Lauren Coles, aged 10
Sharmans Cross Junior School

   WEST MIDLANDS WINNER

Then or Now?

In Victorian times, life was extremely different to modern living today. For one thing, you would have had just one bath a week. Imagine being child number eight – you would have bathed in seven other people's bath water! How unhygienic! As if that wasn't disgusting enough, you had to put on your dirty clothes after your bath again. Yuck!

Children were looked down on. They were of no importance. If you were lucky enough to go to school, and if you didn't behave you were caned, or deliberately humiliated in front of the school. If this wasn't bad enough, most of the teachers hated kids. Your class teacher probably loves kids, and wants to help you to learn and grow up. They wouldn't in Victorian times.

You have probably heard the Dickensian expression, "Children should be seen and not heard." Almost all adults and teachers in Victorian times believed this, and acted as far as possible to make it happen!

Also in Victorian times, if you got the merest little scrape on your hand, after a few short days there would be pus oozing out of it, and you would have no way of stopping or helping it. If you had a simple cut now you would wash it, maybe put some ointment or antiseptic on it then cover it up with a sterile plaster. In Victorian times good hygiene and sterile treatments were only enjoyed by those who were rich.

Children also eat better nowadays. Poor children in Victorian times used to eat about one meal a day, meaning that they were malnourished, suffered from lack of vitamins, and didn't have very much meat or fish at all. All this meant that they didn't have very good concentration or intelligence. Also, for the very poor,

every day's meal was boiled cabbage with cabbage for pudding or something equally awful! Yum.

In 2003 children go to school around the age of three, and leave at eighteen plus. In Victorian times, if you were lucky enough to go to school, you left at the age of twelve, and then were sent to work. Common children's jobs were nursery maids, chimney sweeps and factory workers. If your family was poor, you just skipped the school part and went straight to work. Children were good chimney sweeps as they were small, so could fit up the chimney easily. There was always the horrible prospect of the child being forgotten and a fire being lit in the grate. Ouch.

Hospitals, instead of being nice, caring places, were buildings of horror, blood and often death. There were no proper sterile surfaces, and the beds were probably changed once a month, instead of with each new patient. People often went into the hospital filled with dread, and they were right to be frightened. There were no anaesthetics and germs were spread easily because of all the sickness. Worst of all, rats roamed free, building nests in the equipment stores; they bit and scratched the patients, making their sicknesses and diseases ten times worse. Until Florence Nightingale, almost no one survived a stay in hospital!

So has this changed your mind, or have you stayed with your original opinion? Whatever your answer is, I think you'll all agree that Victorian times were vile.

By Hana Osborne, aged 10
Hebden Royd C of E (VA) School

YORKSHIRE AND HUMBERSIDE WINNER

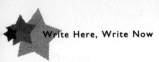

Then or now?

As you can see in the paragraphs above, living conditions 150 years ago weren't fantastic. Nowadays we have hot running water in our homes and INDOOR flushing toilets – we don't have to go out into the cold dark of night. We also have the ability to control how many children we have so our houses aren't cramped. Therefore, that shows you how our living conditions have improved.

Now moving on to transport, children in the Victorian times would not be able to go on holiday to, for example, America, because it would take them months and months to get there. Now we can just jump on a plane with our family and go to America and it would only take about 9 hours!

Now compare that to 150 years ago. What would you rather do?

Nevertheless, more importantly, how about going to have an operation? The majority of operations were very dangerous – many killed people because the doctors were uneducated. Operations relied upon ether or chloroform to make you sleep so you didn't feel the pain – these were later found to damage livers. Now we have anaesthetic and we have special hygienic operating theatres to perform proper operations in. There are also highly qualified doctors/surgeons.

Still with the medical matter, you had to pay to see a doctor. What would happen if, like most Victorian families, your family was poor and you didn't have enough money to pay to be treated? You could die from relatively minor illnesses. Now it is free for everyone to see and be treated by a doctor with the NHS (National Health Service).

Now for your education. Getting a good education is important don't you agree? Otherwise, you will not live a good life after school. This means working hard, but how could you do that if you don't get fresh air? The playgrounds in the Victorian times were inside in a cramped stuffy room. No fresh air equals no hard work. And also if you are going to get a good job then you need to learn about all sorts of subjects, like we do – PE, RE, Science, Maths, English, History, and Geography to name but a few. Alas Victorian boys only learnt maths and English, girls learnt things like sewing and household work. Education leads to a better life.

Still on your education. To be able to learn to a high standard you need to go to school for a reasonable amount of time. You wouldn't have got that if you only went to school for eight years, starting school at the age of five until you were 13 (if you were lucky). When your education finished, you would start hard, low paid work as for example, a chimney sweep or in one of the many workhouses. Pretty tough eh?! Now we are able to go to school for 12+ years, from age five to 16 (it is up to

you after the age of sixteen). There are now universities or colleges available to everyone RICH OR POOR.

The main reason why I prefer to live NOW rather than during the Victorian times is because of the punishment they had. Imagine sitting in your classroom now and getting bored of your lesson, so you decide to flick a piece of paper across the classroom, and you are caught. What is the worst punishment that your teacher would give you? Maybe send you to the head teacher's office, take away your break, shout at you? Well whatever he or she would do is nowhere near as bad as what would happen to you if you did it in the Victorian times, believe me!!!! You would be beaten to a pulp with rulers, canes or even whips.

SO DO YOU _AGREE_ WITH ME? NOW IS A BETTER TIME TO BE ALIVE!!!

By Joanne Woodhams, aged 9
Orchard Way Primary School

LONDON WINNER

Then or Now!

Children in Victorian times weren't really children. They didn't have a childhood. As soon as they could walk many children were sent out to work.

If I was a Victorian child I would most definitely be at work either selling flowers, that I had bought with my penny that morning, or working as a maid in a rich family's house. That would be if I was lucky. I would be regarded as an adult having to earn money to support my family.

I much prefer living nowadays and having fun with my friends or family and not worrying about money or jobs.

If I was born into a rich family in the Victorian times life would be a little bit easier than being poor, but that does not mean to say that I could have fun. I would have to be very well mannered and live in the nursery, which would be where I would be tutored and learn how to sew and play the piano. The only time I would see my parents would be if I was eating a meal with them. But I wouldn't run into the dining room and start telling them about my day, I would walk in and seat myself on a particular seat and wait for the meal to be served. After I had finished my meal I would wait to be excused and then return to the nursery. On the other hand, in reality I have a loving family who cares for me and looks after me. They also listen to my opinions. My home is clean, tidy, spacious and hygienic. Poor Victorian families would share a single room. They would sleep, eat and if they were lucky bath in the same room. If they did have a bath they would have to take turns using the same bath and the same water. The bath would be made out of tin and put in front of a fire. By the time the whole family had been in the bath the water would be very dirty indeed.

In Victorian times children had to pay for their education. If you could afford an education in the Victorian times the teachers would be much stricter, they didn't let you get away with anything! Nearly every child went home with a very sore hand for they would get the dreaded cane for lots of things such as being late for school, blotting your copy book, getting sums wrong and talking out of turn. In my school teachers aren't *that* strict and aren't allowed to use the cane. *Instead they use their voices!* Learning is made to be fun in our days.

Having studied the Victorians I have come to a conclusion that there is nothing in the Victorian time that would attract me to live then. For I enjoy being a child now with a loving family, a comfortable home, a school I enjoy and toys to play with.

By Nicola Hinde, aged 10
Crosby-on-Eden School

NORTH WEST WINNER
NATIONAL WINNER

Think Victorian life was hard? – think again!!!

Life for children in Victorian times was strict, but it must have been easier because whatever rules there were, were made for the children's safety.

Children would have much more freedom and could play out on the street with their friends for as long as they liked. No one would ever worry because they couldn't have been knocked down by motor cars because cars were simply not around. Adults didn't even need to worry about the children watching bad television because it wasn't invented. So they would be outside making up their own games and they would be healthy and fit. I can tell you that for certain.

Who needs central heating when all you have to do is snuggle up to your brother and sisters to keep you warm? You'd probably share a bed with them and you could whisper to them all night, and when you're all awake you could play together with all your toys and then you could go to the shops and buy a loaf of bread with them.

If you were poor, you wouldn't have to go to school which would be really good because you could play all day with your brothers and sisters and no one would tell you off for skipping school. We all know what fun it would be if you didn't need to go to school and you could play all day long. How cool would that be? Compare that to going to boring old school in 2003 and think of all that homework you have to do now! Whereas then, it was no school, no homework! I know what I'd rather do! Being an 1850s child must have been so much fun.

Some of the buildings in the main cities and towns have great architecture and are beautifully decorated with lots of lovely patterns on the roofs. If you see one of these buildings, it may be a Victorian one which has lasted over a century.

You may think "How will I live without a car?" but really it would have been easy because the trains were a great form of transportation. But the most important thing is your children would be healthy because of all the exercise and the fresh air they would be taking in by walking everywhere.

Victorian clothes were so pretty, it didn't matter if you were poor or rich or even worked in a workhouse, they were all pretty whatever they were like and the children had beautiful dolls that were really pretty and I bet you could have had wonderful games with them.

It's up to you what you choose. Would you rather be an 1850s child with all that freedom or would you be in 2003 with no freedom? It's up to you!!!!

By Aisling Culhane, aged 10
St Winefride's Catholic Primary School

EAST MIDLANDS WINNER

Life as a modern child is best!

Firstly, I'm writing to persuade all you children out there that it is better now than to live back then, in fact I'm warning you, please for your safety be persuaded by this text and live now, otherwise goodbye games and gadgets, the Victorians (sadly) didn't have the technology, we do.

Secondly, how would you like to sleep with your little brothers and sisters, for you'd have to sleep with four of them. Just to make matters worse any unpleasant killing diseases or types of sicknesses your family gets I'm 99% sure you'll get too! There were hardly any cures and remember you've got to sleep with them.

If you need the bathroom at 12:00 am then get your slippers on because you're going on a midnight hike, "There's a toilet 50 yards away down the road!" You won't get lost for you can smell it a mile away and it's a game of guess what, when you lift that toilet lid up just to find there's a 5-inch spider underneath. You'll also probably 85% of the time have to go back to get that toilet paper, and with no electricity because they didn't have torches, just an 'easy to go out candle'.

So pitch dark, smelly, risking your life, rolling over your sisters in the middle of the night, no thanks! I'm sure nearly everyone in the world will agree with me.

If you're against pollution, then in the Victorian days 175 years ago wasn't the time to be around. The only thing to cook their food with was a nice, open fire, with black polluting smoke coming out. Even though the Victorians didn't have cars they still burnt rubber!

With all this smoke, there's a million and one diseases you can get, and most of the women and girls out there would have to slave hours over a hot and sweaty, disease-full black smoke which can kill. It's not like having a barbecue today.

Which would you prefer? A nice luxurious bath or a tin, crammed little one. I'll take the luxurious bath!

All you 6 to 9 year olds out there, consider yourself lucky, because as a Victorian normally you'd die at 5. You can live till 100+ now and if you were about to be operated on, then personally I'd rather suffer. We've also got loads of technology like electronic games + ... lots lots more. The Victorians only had an empty road.

You can get brilliant education now, back then only the boys did and even then it wasn't brilliant. And if you think your teacher is strict, then you've got something else coming, in the Victorian days your hands were whipped so much you came out of school with your hands bleeding.

If you ever go to prison, then to the Victorians you'd be living in luxury and if you think prisons are really bad then think again. The only punishment you would get now is community work, back then you'd be tortured, used as a slave or killed. If dog food was invented in the Victorian days, then they'd probably eat it. In prison now you get nice food although you are locked up in a cell so even though I've said what I have, don't go and get yourself arrested!

To conclude I would like to say once again it's better nowadays, imagine back then 12:00 night time, going for an unpleasant hike to the privy 50 yards away after tumbling over the rest of your sick family, then to find there's no toilet paper and then having to sit yourself on that odorous hole with spiders and all sorts of creepies and diseases in there. Would you like to slave over a sweaty fire and then have to stay at home from work because you're uneducated and sick? I think all of you would agree with me (hopefully) it's better nowadays!

By Harry Riddle, aged 10
Fitzmaurice Primary School

SOUTH WEST WINNER

43

Then or Now

The Victorians lived over one hundred and fifty years ago during the reign of Queen Victoria. The quality of life depended on whether you were rich or poor. If you were rich you could have a good and easy life. But if you were poor you could have a rough and hard life, often ending up in the workhouse or early death. People had extra large families. But today nearly everybody is wealthy. Most people today have quite a small family. It is not usual that people have a really big family such as seven or eight children!

Firstly, I wouldn't want to live one hundred and fifty years ago because of the jobs they used to do in the town. Some girls, if they were poor, would go and work at the age of ten. When you were older you would probably be a head maid who dusts the lights and things. You would probably only get one afternoon off in a month. On Mother's Day you would only see your mother on Mother's Day morning. You got one and a half hours free time a day. They started from 6:00 am in the morning and finished at 11:00 pm at night. I can't imagine me getting up that early. When adults needed to do a job they couldn't do they sent a smaller child to do them. They would send smaller boys or girls, mostly boys, up the chimney to clean them. Most of them would have been pulled out dead. Some girls sold flowers, a penny a bunch. There was a big machine which made material. Fluff went down under the table. Little children as young as four would pick the fluff up from beneath the table. They had to be careful not to catch anything on the machine. They didn't stop the machine because that would waste money. In the country the jobs were helping with the harvest, picking crops or potatoes, scaring birds, picking up stones and looking after animals.

Secondly, I would not want to wear Victorian clothes because they look horrible. Rich children dressed the same as their parents. URG!!!!! They were no good for playing in.

Thirdly, school was very strict. If you did anything wrong you would get the cane. If you sulked, spat on somebody or did bad work, here comes the cane! No way! I wouldn't want to go to school in Victorian times.

Next, if you were an orphan, you would end up in the workhouse. If you had no money to look after yourself, you would end up in the workhouse. If you were too old for a job, you would end up in the workhouse. If you couldn't find a job, it's off to the workhouse. The workhouse was like a prison. You hardly got any food. Men there used to crush the bones which had gone rotten, from the pigs. The men were so hungry, they even ate the rotten meat off the bones. Their job was to crush them. I would not want to go there, would you?

Therefore, poor people ate a lot of bread and porridge. They ate few fruit, vegetables and little meat. Rich people ate a lot of good things. In other words, anything they liked. If you lived in the countryside, you ate loads of pig. They would make the pigs fat on purpose. They put the pigs in a small pen, so they couldn't get much exercise. They would make their own sausages and bacon. Pig was the most common meat in Victorian times. People needed a lot of fat for energy. Would you like to eat that?

In addition, toilets would probably be outside in Victorian times. What if it was raining and you needed the toilet? No way!

Next, cars were not invented in those days, therefore you had a carriage. It must have been fun. But can you imagine how slow it would have been and very uncomfortable? Yes, really slow and bumpy!

In conclusion, would I like to live one hundred and fifty years ago, being sent to the workhouse, eating porridge, getting the cane and having to get up at six in the morning? Or would I like to live nowadays and be playing computer games, going everywhere in cars, watching TV and eating burgers? I think I know which ones I would prefer doing. What about you?

By Jade Healey, aged 9
Newton Longville C of E Combined School

   SOUTH EAST WINNER

STORY

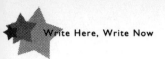

Gillian Cross wrote…

The box didn't come by post.

Sam found it on the doorstep in the morning. It was lying against the door, propped up on one end. When Sam opened the door, the box fell forward, into the house. As it hit the floor, it made a strange noise.

It was a wooden box, about the size of a shoebox, made of plain, unpainted pine. The lid was nailed down and there were two labels stuck across it. FRAGILE said the first one, in big red letters. THIS WAY UP. The letters on the second one were even bigger. THIS PACKAGE MUST BE OPENED IMMEDIATELY.

Sam ran down the hall and unlocked the side door. "Mum! Dad! Wait a minute!" Too late. The car was already pulling away from the garage. As it drove off down the road, the school bus passed it, coming the other way. It was time to leave but the box had to be moved first. It was holding the front door open.

Sam locked the side door and ran back down the hall. At that moment, whatever was inside the box made another noise.

It was much louder this time.

INTRODUCING THE STORIES

The exciting and intriguing story opening from **Gillian Cross** certainly proved stimulating for our young writers. Sam's encounter with the mysterious 'wooden box, about the size of shoebox, made of plain, unpainted pine' set imaginations alight, and inspired a wonderful range of stories. Whether they're out of this world, or closer to home, you always want to know what happens next!

Joe Rolleston's wonderfully inventive story develops a gripping plot with mystery and suspense. The narrator is drawn into a race against time as Sam does battle with computer viruses and emails, offering an intriguing glimpse into a hi-tech future.

In **Jessica Lees'** entry, the readers feel as if they really get to know Sam, the football-kicking heroine of the piece. Her enjoyable asides as she talks to herself lend real personality to the story.

The story from **Thomas Cureton-Fletcher** is a real page-turner. He builds the tension and suspense skilfully and we are left wondering how Sam finally deals with the green-footed monster... In **Sebastian Alexander-Sowa's** imaginative story, Sam is able to turn to a mysterious wizard-like figure with 'piercing green eyes, a long, white beard and a dark, musty cloak' to help him out of his predicament.

An intriguing mixture of past and present is offered by **Chimwemwe Ngoma's** engaging story. Neatly moving between the twenty-first century and the reign of Charles II, readers are left to ponder – was it a dream or reality? In contrast, **Sam Rankin's** story about a 'three-foot mix of an elf and a dwarf' is firmly rooted in the present day, but with a strong element of fantasy. As the story concludes, readers will want to know – what *did* Sam's mother think when she got home?

Anyone who has ever kept a hamster will sympathise with Sam's adventures in **Conor Selvage's** humorous but touching story. His hamster, Ben, certainly has his own personality, and makes an entertaining if unpredictable companion.

Niamh Pearson Cockrill's well-paced story strongly conveys the frustration Sam must have felt when he was prevented time and again from opening the box. His thoughts wander as he wonders what might be in the mysterious package, his anticipation growing as the day goes on...

Elsa Hariades' entry is a poignant story with a chilling edge to it. The reader is left wondering how history might have been different if the parcel had arrived on time, all those years ago. **Alice Ahearn's** story also has a historical angle as the hero takes a trip back in time, and finds himself hard at work in the kitchen of a medieval castle.

Nadia Sousa builds a sense of excitement and anticipation as Sam and his companions struggle to open the box and find out what's inside. His friend ends up in hospital – but did the inhabitant of the box, the 'small man dressed in wizard's clothes', have anything to do with his unfortunate accident?

Time travel features in **James'** inventive story, as our hero is transported to the year 2028 to save the world. With a range of technical trickery, Sam becomes 'the hope for the human race', applauded for his bravery and skill – but it's not long before reality beckons.

Enter The Mainframe

It was a kind of gruff mew, not scary, but eerie.
Sam tapped the side of the package timidly, nothing.
The box was silent.
"I don't like this at all," thought Sam.
He was usually a brave kid, he looked tough, but sometimes things scared him.
By looking tough I mean short, spiked, blond hair and these really 'I'm tough' brown eyes, but really, he was a nice person to know.
As he was about to open the box, a noise came from the computer on the desk behind him.
"I'm sure I shut that down last night ..." said Sam puzzled.
Bleep bleep bleep BLLEEEPPPPPPP!!!!!!!!!!!!!!
That last bleep the PC had emitted was really loud and high-pitched. Then the screen turned blue and a message appeared.

E-Mail from: <u>BlazingUnicorn@ntl.co.Jptr</u>
<u>Read now</u> or <u>save to inbox</u>

Sam grabbed the mouse, but he hadn't a clue who 'BlazingUnicorn' was!
<u>READ NOW</u>. He entered.

To: <u>DarkAngelX@enteel.com</u>
   Are u going 2 open that box any time this year!? Hurry up. Anyway Sam, in there is a powerful plutonic sphere called 'The Omnicron'. It's very, very important and powerful. Take it to <u>ThunderCrown7@hotmail.plt</u>. Mail me if you get stuck.
<u>Save</u> or **<u>Delete</u>**?

"What the ..."
Sam tore the box open and as well as this Omnicron, a small glass sphere, there was a small tiger!
"Grrrrrrrrrrr."

Sam jumped back, and the tiger arched its back.

Bleep

Sorry, forgot to mention Lag, he's an Endomorph, he'll be your bodyguard!

Then the computer closed down and turned off!

"Endomorph?" said Sam, bewildered by what was going on. Lag started to roar and glow blue!

Then the small tiger became a big tiger!
"Greetings master, I am Lag, an Endomorph from Pluto. We should upload ourselves immediately," remarked Lag in a gruff voice.
"You can t-t-*talk!?*" gasped Sam.
"Of course I can talk, and very fluently may I add." Lag seemed proud of this.
"OK, but what do I need you for, and what do you mean, 'upload'?" enquired Sam.
"I mean let's get going to ThunderCrown7's site."
"Huh?" Sam was totally lost.
"The cosmic weapon Omnicron can only be moved from one place to another via digital means," explained Lag.
"The Omnicron didn't come to me digitally, though," said Sam.
"Yes it did, BlazingUnicorn came to your site and downloaded it to your domain." Lag looked at the computer.
"Viruses! Run!!!" roared Lag.
Sam ran to his computer, grabbed the mouse and started to type.
"Activate Firewall!" Sam slammed Enter.

VIRUS DETECTED! FILTERING
FILTERING VIRUS DELETED, DEACTIVATE FIREWALL

"Yeah! Eat that, computer scum!" celebrated Sam.
"Now how do I upload?" asked Sam.

"I'll do that," said Lag. And in a second they were in the Internet!
"I'll lead," said Lag, and he transformed into a giant bat.
"Wow!" said Sam, impressed.

The Internet was a long psychedelic tunnel with doors along it; each door had an E-Mail address on it.
"ThunderCrown7's site isn't too far from here now," said Lag, relieved.
Then a swarm of bee-like creatures came down the tunnel.
"Aargh! Someone thinks we're a virus and –," started Lag.
"Have sent a QueenBee deleter program to destroy us!" ended Sam, horrified!

Sam ran and ran, but Lag tried to fight them off, flailing his leathery wings at the program. They were stinging the Endomorph and deleting his data byte-by-byte!

"I've got it, change into an energy cell, the program will overload!" cried Sam!
And in five seconds flat, there were frazzled bees all over the floor!

Hours later, they arrived at a door reading:
'THUNDERCROWN7 WELCOME'
"Finally!" cheered Sam.
"I'll handle this," said Lag. Then he transformed into a human, and walked in.
10 minutes later, Lag came out, holding a disc.
"This is to say thanks, it has every made computer game on it." Lag handed the disc to Sam.
"What was the Omnicron for, Lag?" asked Sam.
"Well, in a few days' time an intergalactic war will begin and the allies, Jupiter and Pluto, will need the Omnicron to make sure the war doesn't do any damage to non-fighting planets," explained Lag.
"Right, but why give me the Omnicron, am I the '*Chosen one*' or something?" asked Sam.

"That's simple, you looked a bit bored!" laughed Lag.
"Why you little – well I *was* getting bored!" chuckled Sam.
Sam said goodbye to Lag and set off back home.
Although when he got back he got grounded for leaving
the house!!!!!!!

By Joe Rolleston, aged 10
Wilnecote Junior School

WEST MIDLANDS WINNER
JOINT NATIONAL WINNER

The Beep In The Box

It beeped madly as if it was disturbed by its enclosure. Sam lifted the lid, but at that instant the phone rang. Sam shrugged and jammed the lid back on. She placed the box in the silent basement. It beeped madly again. The piercing noise rang through her head.

"Sam!" her mother shouted down the phone, "I don't want you playing with Tom and Joe. I have had enough of muddy football gear." She hung up.

The telephone rang shrilly again. "Coming to play footie?" Tom asked. "I ... I ... well," she coughed nervously, desperately trying to think what to say, "I'm ill, my throat is sore, I've got a headache and – " Sam slammed down the phone and cut Tom's reply off.

Sam went back to have a look at the box – it was empty! Sam panicked – a feeling she wasn't used to. She was on her own without her parents and a weird 'thing' was loose in the three storey house. "Stop fluttering around like a headless chicken – grow up!" she yelled at herself. Grow up grow up. The words echoed in her head. "Calm yourself," she whispered. Usually Sam would have enjoyed being on her own, but these problems seemed to weigh her down – the box, and the conversation with Tom. She was not enjoying this at all.

Sam set to work to look for the thing. She was expecting it to be an easy task as she thought she would hear it – but the house was silent. She became intrigued with the task. She didn't stop to eat ... it became a mission. Her long black hair swung over her shoulder. "Note to self," she laughed to herself for a moment, "Make an appointment for a hair cut."

Frantically she searched her bedroom. She felt a sharp tug at her hair – she whipped round. Nothing was there. "Ow!" she screamed, as she reached up to rub her head. A metal crab clung to her hair. It beeped madly. Sam ran helplessly to the kitchen, her head tilted to one side from the weight of the crab. The telephone's ear-splitting ring filled the whole house. "Sam, I'm worried about you," Tom's alarmed voice came through the ear piece.

"Tom! Thank goodness you called," Sam looked round to check that no-one was listening. "I have a metal crab clinging to my hair, my parents are out and I just need help!"

The noise of the doorbell echoed through the empty house, Sam ran, charging towards the door like a whirlwind. She flung open the door – breathless.
"Oh Tom! I'm really pleased to see you, this thing is driving me nuts!" Sam moaned.

"Right!" Tom straight away took charge of the situation. He tugged at the heap of metal. Samantha screamed. He tugged again. Sam whimpered. "Sam, shut it!" He tried again, but this time he gently tickled the crab under its belly. The claws immediately let go of Sam's hair and fell to the ground. It flipped on to its back, legs waving in the air.

"SAM! Give it a boot, you know what a powerful kick you have ..." Tom urged Sam. She slowly came forward and took aim, her foot poised to kick. She pulled her leg back and kicked the crab hard. It flew towards the wall where it shattered into tiny shards. There was a strange high-pitched bleeping sound. The noise was unbearable – it shrieked and wailed. Within a few seconds it stopped. The shock of the silence hit the two children, and their stomachs churned.

Tom smiled down at Sam, "That was some kick," he said, "Come on let's go and play footie!"

By Jessica Lees, aged 10
Dunmow St Mary's Primary School

  EAST OF ENGLAND WINNER

Fragile?

Chapter I
The Intruder

Sam pushed the box aside, trying to ignore it. He purposefully walked out of the house, but the box had moved onto the windowsill, and he was being watched, he could sense it.

School that day was fairly normal. As usual Mrs Coden taught them and nothing was wrong, until he was on his way home. He felt strange, as if he had forgotten something and it was mysteriously cold and lonely. He was walking down the almost unfamiliar street, everything was enigmatically silent. No cars drove by, no people strolled past, the only thing that could be heard was the whistling wind. He opened the gate and walked up the path to his house. The front door was slightly open, suspended on one hinge and the box had moved, but where?

Chapter II
Caged

He cautiously walked up to the swinging door and stepped into the hallway.

It was dark, really dark and it was colder than it was outside. The air smelt dank and a faint shuffling noise was resonating upstairs.

But the mysterious thing was that everything was horizontally inverted. Sam stared motionless in disbelief and horror. He stood rooted to the spot, not wanting or willing to move. It felt like blood was rushing to his head, he almost fainted.

Suddenly, a crash echoed through the hallway. It sounded like it came from Sam's bedroom. He didn't want to go upstairs, but something made him and he was literally dragged up onto the landing, trying to restrain himself. The landing was slightly lighter than the hallway, because long, thin dust motes streamed across the room. A large, pine chair was wedged against Sam's door and something was knocking and banging it – the box. He hadn't the nerve to go in, so he tentatively edged up to the door and peered under.

His room was hardly recognisable. He wasn't even positive that it was his room. Something was right at the other side of the door. A shadow slid across the wall and a cavernous padding of feet reverberated through the room.

Suddenly, SMASH! The landing window shattered into diamonds of glass, but how? He automatically raced downstairs to the front door, but it was closed and locked. He was locked in with the creature, and he couldn't escape.

Chapter III
The Weapon

Another crash resounded upstairs. The chair had given way and so had the door.

Something was walking on the landing. Terrifyingly, a small green foot appeared at the top of the stairwell.

Sam froze, for what seemed like an hour, but in reality was seconds. Suddenly, it struck him, like a bolt of lightning.

He tore into the living room, slammed the door behind

him and rolled the sofa in front of it. The creature repeatedly, persistently hammered the blocked entrance. Immediately, a muscular fist penetrated through the door panel. It cracked and the handle turned. Sam firmly gripped it and turned it anti-clockwise, but it was excruciatingly hard. Eerily, everything fell silent, apart from the audible tip, tap, tip, tap of the creature pacing. It sounded like it was going down the hallway, towards the kitchen. He heard it searching the cutlery drawer.

Chapter IV
The Beginning of the End

It had grabbed something, probably a knife to make a hole in the door. And then he heard it walking back up the hallway, getting closer and closer. The creature thrust the steel knife into the door, narrowly missing Sam's head. It was forced through the wooden barrier again and again and again.

Sam frantically searched the room for a weapon, but found nothing. Gradually the door began to open ...

By Thomas Cureton-Fletcher, aged 10
Sitwell Junior School

   **YORKSHIRE AND HUMBERSIDE WINNER**

A Crucial Decision

Sam ran breathlessly to his bedroom, clutching the mysterious box. Even though he knew there was no one else in the house, Sam closed the door carefully behind him just in case. Anxiously and very gently, he placed the box onto his bedside table. Not a sound could be heard, except the constant, rhythmic ticking of the old grandfather clock in the hall below. He stared intently at the strange parcel as though waiting for something to happen. A tingling sensation rippled through him as he eagerly anticipated unleashing the contents of the box.

TICK! TOCK! TICK! TOCK! The monotonous beat of the clock was really starting to get on his nerves. He needed complete silence to really take in the power of this unique package.

As he finally plucked up the courage to approach the magical object, he nervously reached out and began to lift the lid ...

A blinding shaft of light burst from within the box. The lid continued to open of its own accord wider and wider until finally it floated smoothly and landed on the floor of Sam's room.

By now the dazzling white light filled every corner of Sam's bedroom. As he tried to shield his eyes, Sam risked a peek into the once seemingly normal box. What he saw before him made his mouth drop open in awe ...

At first he was convinced that it was some kind of illusion. But as he took time to inspect the source of the light, he noticed a definite luminous, translucent, beetle-like shape in the heart of the box. Suddenly, he noticed a folded piece of paper on the carpet. He picked it up carefully, unfolded it and read the note. Its enormous looped handwriting said:

The power of this creature is so immense, it has the ability to change all things completely. Do not use the contents of this box without thinking, for incredible things will happen.

While he was not looking, the beetle had escaped from the box. Sam walked silently behind it. It was almost as if it wanted him to follow. Suddenly, it turned around and lifted up its front legs as though asking to be carried. Sam picked it up, and as he did so, there was a blinding flash of light.

Sam caught sight of a wizened figure holding a knobbled, old walking stick. He had piercing green eyes, a long, white beard and a dark, musty cloak. His straight, white moustache bristled as he spoke.

"The creature you hold has powers you could never dream of. Do not use this in haste, for when you unleash the powerful magic of the beetle, there will be no going back..."

As the figure finished speaking, Sam saw the familiar flash of blinding light. The words of the mysterious figure were still fresh in his mind. He was now very reluctant to use the power of this mysterious creature. His brain urged him on, but his heart refused to listen. He was at a crossroads of decision, not knowing which way to turn.

Suddenly, he remembered the stranger's prophecy and he felt a warmth building up inside him. He didn't have to decide now. He could wait another year, a decade or until any time in the future.

An uncontrollable shiver prickled down Sam's spine. He could hear the wind whistling and howling outside. The curtains began flapping noisily. Sam began to feel deeply affected by everything that had happened to him in this small space of time.

The fear was really starting to grip him, like a pair of sharp clawed hands scraping and scratching at him. He felt so terrified he almost wanted to hide from this changing power.

A thick, dense fog seemed to cover all of his room and the world beyond. The dim shadows of the forest stretched out to meet Sam's house. Sam let out a high-pitched shriek. The petrified scream echoed throughout the house. He couldn't take it any more. He couldn't take the chance ...

"I CAN'T DO IT!!!" screamed Sam. The words rebounded off every wall.

Sam sprinted towards his bed, snatched up the treacherous box and thrust it out of the window with all his might. A dazzling burst of light blinded him as the box was blown to smithereens.

Sam felt a great load had been lifted off his mind.

Meanwhile, the creature that had caused so much trouble, scuttled under the fence and slid under the door, looking for its next eager victim ...

By Sebastian Alexander-Sowa, aged 10
St Thérèse of Lisieux School

   NORTH EAST WINNER

SAMANTHA'S ASSIGNMENT

Sam picked up the box and crept gingerly into her room. She placed the box gently on her bed. Sam looked at the calendar on the wall; today was the 2nd of September! She felt her stomach leap. Was *this* the box the old woman had promised?

It had all started when her history teacher had given them an assignment to research information on the Great Fire of London. Samantha had been intrigued by the fact that the fire had started in the bakery of King Charles II!

After school she had hurried down to a little, old bookshop. She was reading about the colourful character of King Charles II and his love of money and women when an old plump lady unexpectedly appeared. Samantha had asked her for information. The old lady had given her strange advice with an even stranger request. On 2nd September Samantha would receive a box to help her with her research, she must use this on the condition that she returns a lost sapphire ring given to the old woman by King Charles II!

Sam glanced at her watch. She had already missed an hour of school! She wished her parents were there. Apprehensively she prised open the lid and peered inside. It wasn't full of books as she had expected but tools, bits and pieces. Suddenly, without warning they all shot up in the air knocking Sam over. She sat up and watched them form into a big square with a circle in it. Within the circle, numbers appeared just like a clock face.

A voice echoed around the room.

"Samantha
To the future, present or past,
You can get there pretty fast.

Wherever you want to be,
You can get there, just come with me."

"What's going on?" asked Samantha. "How do you know my name? What are you playing at?"

"This is not a game,
I just know your name,
All you need to know
Is where you want to go."

A time machine! At this point the clock face opened like a door. Sam made up her mind she was going back to 1666 and stepped in! There was a loud bang and all she could see were bright colours swirling in front of her. They started to get darker.

She suddenly found herself in a moonlit alley. The night air felt warm and oppressive. Something ran over her foot, a giant rat raced off into the darkness. Samantha choked as nauseating smells hit her. It was then that she remembered 1666 wasn't just the year of the Great Fire but also of the Great Plague!

An old lady in torn and dirty clothes staggered up to her from the shadows. Some of her teeth were missing. "Not lost are ya' ma' dear?" asked the old lady grabbing at Sam.

Terrified, Sam pulled away and ran down into a small cobbled lane. She was watching with horror a family grieving over the body of a small child when she heard a loud, crackling sound. She looked up in astonishment to see the sign Farriner's Bakery! "That's where the fire started!" gasped Sam. And it seemed it already had.

Suddenly she heard a piercing scream. Someone was trapped! Sam rushed over to the bakery and pushed the door open. A blast of hot air hit her. Peering through the thick smoke Sam saw the body of a lady on the floor. She rushed over but the woman wasn't breathing. She was dead! The heat was intense; Sam was about to leave when she noticed the sapphire ring on the lady's second finger. The old woman's request! Hesitantly Sam removed the ring and ran outside. People were screaming, flames licked nearby houses.

Feeling helpless and sad and more than a little tired she headed for the time machine. Its door opened. Then as Sam stepped in, it shuddered and the ring fell with a clink onto the road. It rolled down into a murky drain. All of a sudden everything went black.

"Sam!" called a voice. Sam opened her eyes. It was Mum. "Come on sweetie, you've been asleep for ages, you'll be late for school." She must have been dreaming!
At breakfast, Mum said, "You know that site where they're building those apartments. Apparently they've found a sapphire ring dating back to 1666. It seems the ring survived the Great Fire!"

Sam smiled, maybe it wasn't a dream after all. She must tell the old woman in the bookshop!

By Chimwemwe Ngoma, aged 9
Highfield Junior School

LONDON WINNER

68

The Menace Of The Box

Sam was worried, there were two minutes until the school bus left and he still hadn't found a place to put this stupid box! So he hastily shoved it in the lounge cupboard.

He dashed outside urgently, shouting with all his might. "WAIT! WAIT!" Too late. The engine roared and it whizzed off towards Ugly Manner Primary School. Sam sighed and then gloomily plodded off towards his bike. This box had already earned him detention.

It was another bad day at school.

Sam rode home grumpily on his bike. His mum and dad wouldn't be in, so hopefully he could nick a few toffees at home. What he saw when he opened the front door was beyond imagination. The hall was a disaster! The framed pictures had fallen, the radiator was chipped and the wallpaper was peeling!

Sam's heart was racing. Suddenly, a huge crash could be heard above. Sam thought it must be coming from his bedroom. He raced up the stairs and could not believe what he saw! There was a massive mess; the bed was completely ruined, his computer lay smashed on the floor, the window pane was shattered while rain water was dripping lazily through a hole in the roof.

But strangely enough, there was the box, untouched, unharmed. Then suddenly, the cupboard door clicked ... Sam thought he was hearing things, but ... It clicked again ... Sam's heart was violently punching his stomach, he knew he wasn't hearing things now. As white as a vampire, scarcely breathing, he backed up against the wall. Slowly, the mottled green cupboard door creaked open. Sam's eyes bulged with pure horror. Suddenly, a green flash whizzed out.

Sam screamed, but then turned bright red with embarrassment. There, in front of his very eyes, was the most peculiar creature he had ever seen. It was standing right in front of him, saluting. "Nuzzy at your service, sir!" it squeaked with a high-pitched tone.

Sam could hardly believe his eyes. This wasn't the ten-foot abominable wolf he was expecting! This was a three-foot mix of an elf and a dwarf, dark green warty skin stretched over his bones and bulging facial features, only wearing a paper bag.

"Sorry to desert you, but there is work to be done." Nuzzy whizzed out the door and into the upstairs hall. "WAIT, WAIT!" Sam bellowed, just as he had to the school bus earlier. Questions cycled his mind like a wheel: What is this creature? Where is he from? Why is he here? Little did he know that his questions were about to be answered . . .

He chased Nuzzy into the hall, only to find Nuzzy's trailing leg disappear into his mum and dad's bedroom. He ran into the bedroom and found Nuzzy bouncing on his parent's king-sized bed! Then Nuzzy bounced onto his mum's dressing table, picked up the mirror and was about to throw it onto the floor. This was mum's prized possession! It cost a fortune and she cared for it like a baby. Sam was speechless. He could hardly do a thing to stop Nuzzy now.

Out of his mouth finally came, "Don't do it Nuzzy!" Nuzzy squeaked back, "But Nuzzy must! It is Nuzzy's culture from the Chaos Mountain in Russia. I is one of the many Spartaks who have lived there for generations. It is our will and our destiny to break things forever more!" Then, before Sam could speak, SMASH! Nuzzy giggled and slipped through Sam's legs out into his father's study.

Sam groaned. In here was dad's most prized possession, the XP2005 computer with all the latest software and technology. Nuzzy jumped onto the desk. Sam knew and was dreading what would come next. Nuzzy picked up the computer and was about to throw it when Sam had a brilliant idea! He saw the box lying on the floor and wondered why it was there. But no time for that now! He swiped the box when Nuzzy wasn't looking and picked up his dad's large desktop lamp. Sam shouted, "Hey, Nuzzy! Put the computer down and look what I've got! A large lamp for you to break and smash all you want! It's yours, here, take it!" Nuzzy cheered and slowly walked towards Sam. Just as he was about to grab the lamp Sam quickly stuffed him into the box and shut the lid. "Got you!" shouted Sam.

All the shouts and screams from the box were muffled as Sam wore a triumphant grin. Sam strapped the box up and got on his bike with Nuzzy in the box. He rode off towards the nearest lake. He picked up Nuzzy's box and put it down in the lake and let it drift away. The last he heard was Nuzzy squeaking, "I'll get you for this!" Sam looked at his watch and saw the time – half past five. His mum should have been home five minutes ago! What was she going to say about all this?!!

By Sam Rankin, aged 10
St Mary's CE Primary School

NORTH WEST WINNER

71

Friendship Forever

Sam did not know what to do with the box. So he took it to school and asked his friends to help him open the box. His friends tugged away at the box, but it wouldn't open. Sam asked his teacher to help, but she was nowhere to be seen.

When he got home Sam asked his Mum, but she was busy cooking. He asked his Dad, but he was on his way to the shops. Sam nearly lost his temper because no-one would help him open the box. He was desperate to know what was inside it.

The next morning came and Sam could not open the box. He asked his Dad again, his Dad was able to open the box. A little fluffy hamster was in there. Sam shouted "Mum! Dad opened the box and there's a hamster in it. I don't know what to do with it."
"Keep it!" his Mum called back, so he did.

The next day came and Sam and his Mum went to the pet store and bought food, a cage and lots of other hamster stuff. Sam decided to call his hamster Ben. Sam and Ben had a blast together; they were the best of friends.

One day Sam went to feed Ben, but Ben wasn't in his cage. Ben was gone. The door was open, his wheel was on the floor and his food bowl was upside down.

Sam thought he knew where Ben was. So Sam looked on the stairs, but he was surprised to see that Ben wasn't on the stairs. He looked in the bath and he saw Ben. Ben was rolling backwards and forwards on his little skateboard.

Ten years passed, Sam was 19 years old and Ben was 10 years old. Ben was still alive, but extremely fluffy

Story

and fuzzy. Sam decided to cut Ben's fluff off and leave him with some hair.

The next morning came after the haircut. Sam gave Ben some food, fresh water and treats. Ben was still asleep.

Two more years passed. Ben did not have the strength to skateboard in the bath anymore, but he could still get out of his cage. Sam was nearly 21 years old and Ben was nearly 12 years old.

One morning Sam woke up and went down to see Ben. Ben was not in his cage and the cage door was open, Ben was gone.

Sam began searching the house for Ben. He remembered the time many years ago when he found Ben in the bath. He looked in the bath; there was no Ben, only his skateboard.

Sam continued looking downstairs and noticed that the cupboard was open and spied some of Ben's hamster food. Sam went into the cupboard and was surprised to see the box that Ben came in was open. As he peered into the box he saw Ben curled up into a little ball of fluff. Sam felt a tear run down his face. He knew Ben wasn't asleep.

By Conor Selvage, aged 9
James Wolfe Primary School

73

AWARDS FOR IMPROVEMENT JOINT WINNER

What's inside the box?

Sam approached the mysterious package and carefully but quickly slipped it into his backpack. He slung the bag over his shoulder and rushed to the bus.

What could it be?
Where did it come from?

At the very back of the bus was Sam's favourite spot. So he sat down and opened his bag. He took the box out cautiously and laid it on his lap. Curiously he read the labels again and grabbed the top of the secret chest and pulled the top.

SCREECH! The bus came to a sharp halt. A sudden jolt nearly made Sam drop the box; quickly he pushed the box back into the bag and jumped off the bus. "Maybe I can open it in the cloakroom?" Sam thought so he ran into the cloakroom and hung up his coat. Then he slowly crouched down and put his arm round his bag making sure nobody could see. He turned his head from left to right checking nobody was there.
DING-A-LING-A-LING! The bell chorused.

Sam jumped up startled, dropping his books and his bag; he knelt down, gathered all the books and ran to class.

Sam sighed and whispered to himself, "Will I ever open that box?" then took a deep breath and walked to his desk. He sat down and pulled out his homework (scruffy like usual) and handed it in.

Even though art and English were his favourite subjects he couldn't concentrate, all he thought about was the box.

74

DING-A-LING-A-LING! The bell yet again echoed down the corridor.

"Yes!" Sam thought, "this is my chance to open that box!"

"Class you may go to lunch," said Mrs Bell whilst marking their homework.

Sam ran like thunder to the door, pushing and knocking people over in a desperate attempt to get to the cloakroom before anyone else.

In the cloakroom there were piles of gym kit and coats scattered all over the floor. Pushing and digging his way through the pile he finally reached his bag. He flicked it open, put his hand in and pulled out the wooden box. Sam sneakily tip toed into the boys' toilets clutching the box securely.

This was it.

CREAK! The box opened. A big excited smile grew on Sam's face. Sam held his breath and closed his eyes. CREAK! He opened the box a bit further then he opened his eyes. Sam could have fainted with disappointment, his big excited grin drooped into a sad frown. It was a knitted jumper. Dismayed Sam covered his face with his hands, slumped onto the bench and gave out a very loud sigh.

"It must have been the button scratching against the top of the box that made the noise. Well I might as well put it on," shrugged Sam. It was a perfect fit so he went home in his new red spotty jumper.

DING-DONG-DING-DONG the bell rang. Sam rushed downstairs and opened the door to greet the guest. It was his grandma. The kettle shook from side to side vigorously. Sam picked it up and poured a cup of tea for him and grandma.
"Did you get my package, the one with the woolly jumper?" asked Sam's grandma.
"Unfortunately yes," muttered Sam under his breath.

By Niamh Pearson Cockrill, aged 10
The Elms Junior School

EAST MIDLANDS WINNER
JOINT NATIONAL WINNER

76

Sam's Mystery Parcel

Sam was in a panic. She had no idea what to do with the box. In a hurry to get to school, she stuffed the box into her bag thinking it was her lunch and hurried out of the front door, slamming it behind her.

Sam sat daydreaming all through maths and English. She finally heard the caretaker ring the bell for lunch and she joined the rush to get out of the classroom door.

Seated in the dining hall, Sam stared at the box in front of her. This was not her familiar brown lunch box. At once Sam realised her mistake. In her haste to catch the bus she had put the box – the one which had arrived on the doorstep that morning – in her bag thinking it was her lunch.

She reread the message on the lid of the box – "OPEN IMMEDIATELY". She was dying to see what was inside but didn't want to attract the attention of the other children sitting at the table.

"Would you mind if I went outside for a minute Miss Essex. I'm feeling a bit faint," she said to the dinner lady. "Not at all Sam," replied Miss Essex, kindly.

Sam felt a surge of excitement as she went out into the playground. She found a nice quiet corner where she could open the box undisturbed.

Just at that moment the box made a curious sound, which seemed to be coming from inside. It was a faint whistling sound, which made Sam feel uneasy.

"Well, here goes," she said under her breath, as she slowly and nervously removed the lid of the dusty box.

Inside the box Sam saw to her surprise a collection of objects, which looked very old. There was a photograph of a young girl of about Sam's age wearing what Sam knew to be Victorian clothes. The box also contained a small green tin which when Sam opened it revealed a crusty piece of bread, a small chunk of cheese and an apple.

"How strange," thought Sam.

Just then the bell rang for the end of lunch so Sam hastily replaced the lid on the box and made her way back inside.

The afternoon seemed to drag on really slowly. Sam had decided to go to the local museum after school for she knew this must be a very old box.

As soon as school had finished, Sam rushed outside and quickly made her way to the town museum. When she got inside she managed to find her way to the Victorian section, a dark cold room filled with objects, photos and paper with lots of writing on, all in shiny glass cabinets. She scanned around the room looking for evidence and clues which might relate to the mysterious box.

She walked over to the photo section. She was just about to leave that part when a photo right at the bottom caught her eye. Sam recognised it but why?
Of course! That was exactly the same as the one in the box.

"Excuse me," Sam said to the museum assistant, "do you know anything about this girl?"
"Only that she died at the famous mill explosion of 1846. A young girl she was, only 11 years old, about your age I would guess."
"Wow! Thanks," Sam said.
"1846" Sam thought to herself, maybe they had more information about this girl.

She searched the paper section. There were lots of letters written on old crumpled up yellow paper, one of them with the same date that the museum assistant had mentioned:

24th June 1846

Dear Molly

Please do not go to work today. It is far too dangerous. Yesterday as I was working at the mill, I noticed the faint smell of gases and I fear today it could be worse. I will not be at work today as mother is taking us all on a family treat. Please use my whistle to warn other workers if something is wrong.

With much love
    Your best friend
    Jessica Frankford xxx

Sam looked at her watch. "5.30," she gasped, "Mum'll be furious!!"

She ran out of the museum and sprinted back home.

At home, Sam opened the box but this time she noticed an old battered whistle. She picked it up and examined it. As she did so she felt a strange and rather sinister feeling. Did Molly ever receive the letter that could have saved her life and possibly many others?

Sam would never know.

By Elsa Hariades, aged 10
Exbourne C of E Primary School

SOUTH WEST WINNER

The Time Package

It was a kind of whirling noise, like the sound of an approaching hurricane. Sam made up his mind in a split second. He hurried down into the cellar and started rummaging around in a cupboard for his dad's crowbar. He was uncomfortably aware, as he pulled and tugged at the crowbar, that time was ticking on and the school bus would be waiting for him. When it eventually came loose, to his dismay, a whole lot of other stuff came tumbling out with it, and it took at least ten minutes to get everything neatly piled back into the cupboard.

Sam summoned up the little courage he had and sprinted back up the cellar steps, the toots of the bus's horn sounding ten times louder to his ears than they really were. He skidded to a halt in the front doorway, picked up the box (which was surprisingly light considering its size) and took it into the kitchen. Prising the lid off wasn't easy, especially due to the fact that his hands were trembling with a mixture of nerves (what would his teacher say when he arrived twenty minutes late?) and apprehension (what could possibly be so fragile that it was covered in warning labels and packaged in a wooden box?). The lid finally flew off, with such tremendous force that it skimmed across the kitchen tiles and hit the wall in a shower of splinters. Sam flinched as flakes of paint crumbled off the wall – his dad had only painted it a week ago – but his attention soon strayed to the box. It was empty.

Except –

BANG!

Sam's hair stood on end as the kitchen filled with howling wind and swirling colour. Papers in Mum's in-tray slid off the counter and started rocketing around

81

the room, the pot of cutlery fell over and sent the knives, forks and spoons bouncing along the tiles, a huge hurricane swallowed Sam up...

Bump.

"Ouch!"

Land hard. Stand up. Gasp. Servant gear!

He gasped again when he saw his surroundings. He was in the kitchen of a medieval castle! He was about to look for assistance when a cook brushed past him, dangling some dead chickens by their legs.

"Er, sorry ..."

"Couldn't pluck these for me, James, could yah?" asked the cook in a rough, servanty way. "I've gotta go and catch some more."

Sam stared after her as she hurried downstairs. This cook thought he was a totally different person – a kitchen hand, by the sound of things. He knew the servants would be furious if he disobeyed them, so he walked stiffly over to the low trestle table and started to pluck the chickens. He had always been squeamish, and his nerves were not exactly up for plucking greasy chickens. He was then told to go and draw some water. This was no easier. Every step he took seemed to make the bucket get heavier.

"Took long enough, dincha?!" remarked the cook. "Now, clear off."

Sam cleared off.

He saw a set of stone steps outside the door of the cavernous kitchen. He proceeded upstairs, blinking in the bright sunlight. He found he was in a large courtyard. The lower bailey was packed with people wandering round, and echoing with merchants yelling at passers-by, advertising their wares.

But he didn't have much time to take in the scenery, because people were treading on his bare feet. He scuttled into a small hut selling dyed cloth. Here, it wasn't so crowded. He would stay behind the dye vat until he could figure out what to do. He sat down on a sack of unused cloth.

If I got here, he thought, by opening a box that makes funny noises, that's well enough, but how do I get out? Surely the same circumstances couldn't arise again.

But then, he remembered that he'd stuffed the box inside his sweater just as he'd been eaten by the hurricane. He felt around under his tunic, found it, and wrenched it out. Somehow, it had managed to acquire another lid. Sam cast around for something to open it and his eyes alighted on a nearby woodchip. He stuck it under the lid and shoved.

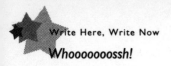

Whooooooooossh!

"Sam!"

Sam's mum was towering above him, apoplectic.

"Yes?"

"Don't speak to me like that!" spat his mum, sparks flying from her eyes. "Why aren't you in school?"

"Oh, I got sidetracked."

Sam's mum exploded at him. Sam didn't care, though. He grinned. That just brought things back to normal.

By Alice Ahearn, aged 10
Holy Trinity CE Junior School

 SOUTH EAST WINNER

84

The Present

Sam was worried. He didn't know what to do with that box. The noises were making him even more worried. Then he thought of bringing it in to school because he didn't want to leave it there. So pling! ... he put the box in his bag and off he went.

In class he got into trouble with the teacher because she thought Sam was making rude noises. But it was the box, squeaking and growling.

When he got home, his parents weren't in. He put the box under his bed and went down to make his own tea. He decided to call his friends because he felt a bit scared to open the box on his own. Fifteen minutes later they were there, his best friends Alan and Leila.

They looked at the box. It was quiet, now.
"It's just a boring box, Sam. What did you call us round here for that for?" said Alan.
"No wait," said Sam. He took a deep breath. "It's not just a simple box. It makes strange and scary noises."
They both laughed at him and Sam felt a bit silly. Leila picked up the box and shook it hard. Nothing. Then she threw it over to Alan. He caught it and they both had a game of catch.
"Stop it," said Sam, "there was a noise, there was."
"Well, there's nothing now." Said Alan, laughing. "You're getting a bit crazy, Sam I think."

Then a little high whining noise came from the box. Then some strange clicks and a rattle. Leila was holding the box. She was so shocked. She dropped the box on her foot. "OW!" she screamed. Alan stopped laughing straightaway. They all stared at the box. Leila sat down holding her foot.
"That was a mean trick, Sam," she said. "I think my toe

85

is broken." She took off her trainer and sock. Her big toe was getting bigger and bigger. It looked sore and red. Alan stared at Sam and then back at the box.

"See!" said Sam.

"What do you think it is?" said Alan. He sounded a bit scared now.

"I don't know," replied Sam. "It was squeaking and whining all day at school."

"Maybe it's some kind of animal," said Leila.

"We should let it out then," said Alan.

"No way, it could be dangerous," Leila sounded scared too.

They all looked at the box for a few minutes. Then Alan said, "Well, someone has to open it." He got down on the floor and pulled at it. It was too hard. He picked it up and put it on the table by Sam's window. He picked up the scissors lying on the table and started to cut into the box. The box suddenly started shaking madly, a strange howling noise coming from it. Alan began to feel weak and scared. He tried to let go of the box, but something seemed to be holding his hands to it like glue. He tried to shake it off. He was really scared now. "Help me get rid of it," he cried. Sam and Leila grabbed a side of the box and pulled but it would not leave Alan.

Alan was now really terrified. The noise from the box was getting louder and louder. It was shaking so hard, it was making him jump around the room. He went to the open window and tried to drop it out, trying to shake it out of his arms. But it would not let go. It seemed to squeeze his arms harder and harder. Alan leaned right out of the window and tried to shake the box off as hard as he could.

Sam and Leila could not see exactly what happened. But they heard Alan scream. The next minute he was gone. Sam walked slowly over to the window, too scared nearly to look out. But he did and saw Alan lying on the ground below.

Next thing, his parents arrived home, called an ambulance and Alan went to hospital. He was alive but badly hurt. The box was still unopened on the path.

Sam's dad picked it up. "What was Alan doing?" he said.
"Trying to open the box," said Sam.
Sam's dad pulled open the box. It opened easily. Sam's mum looked inside.
"Oh," she said, "I think it must be a present for you Sam, probably from Grandma. It's a very old toy that she had when she was little. She was talking about giving it to you."
She lifted the object out of the box.

It was a figure – a small man dressed in wizard's clothes; a tall hat with stars on, a long dress with the same pattern.
"It's clockwork," said Mum. "You wind it up and it waves its wand. She wanted to give it to me when I was little but it always scared me. How silly is that!"

Sam stared at the toy. It was looking at him he thought.

"After all," said his mum, "what danger is there from a little toy!"

By Nadia Sousa, aged 10
Haseltine School

A.D: The Hope for the Human Race

Sam was dying to know what was in that box. So he got out of his dad's tool box a small hammer. Using his muscles, he pulled the nails out. He opened the wooden lid and took out a small metal tube. As if by magic, he dropped it and the tube grew enormous. He went inside the tube, wondering what to do. Then, like the voice of a computer, the tube seemed to say "Greetings Soldier! You have gone into the year 2028 postal tube."

The tube sucked Sam up like a powerful vacuum cleaner. He fell onto a metal floor. A walking computer on legs with white arms and cartoonish gloves walked over to Sam.

"Greetings human life form. You have now reached the year 2028. Get into that tube," said the walking computer, pointing to a tube about the size of a modern wooden door. There popped out from the ceiling metal arms with pincers on the end. They carried Sam from the floor and dropped him in the tube.

"Don't worry, this won't hurt a bit," said the computer.

Something like an electric shock touched him! Sam's hand seemed to transform. An explosion of smoke came out of the tube. Sam found himself covered in powerful weapons of mass destruction. His hair was longer. On his shoes were hidden pockets out of which came missiles. There were suckers on the soles of his shoes.

"You are now A.D, the hope for the human race. You have amazing powers and you are totally indestructible, fast and manoeuvrable," said the walking computer.

"How can I do all these things?" said Sam excitedly.

"Read the manual," said the walking computer, and gave him a manual so heavy, even the strongest man in the world couldn't lift it.

When Sam (who we should now call A.D), started reading the manual – which was about 2,450 pages long, he had trouble turning over the pages. So, the metal arms with pincers on helped him. By the time he'd finished reading it, it was 9.00 pm. When he wanted to go to bed, he said to the metal arms with pincers (who you must not forget), "I want to go to bed." The metal arms vanished and out came blow lamps, screwdrivers and other sorts of tools. They all started making a bed, and it only took 1½ seconds to make.

Sam got into bed. The next morning he heard something which he thought was his alarm clock. He got out of bed and fell down clumsily. He shook all the stars out of his head and found that his imaginary alarm clock was red sirens which were louder than the loudest voice in Madam Butterfly.

Somebody's voice on a megaphone was shouting: "Run for your life, there's a meteor coming!" In the lab where he had landed, two armed robots with a machine gun and wicked bat-like wings started shooting the generations. Before he even knew what he was doing, Sam hit a button on his helmet where a small computer was hanging out, which looked like a Gameboy. The computer showed him a picture of the arch enemy Meteorbots who are kept by the evil Space Ruler, Mayor Meteor. Before he even knew what he was doing, a gun shot out of Sam's hand. I forgot to mention that his hands were also portals for small shrinking tools. He shot a Meteorbot and it sent him into a button which shot a weapon of mass destruction. It sent a large bullet flying into the air, which hit that meteor dead.

Outside, everybody clapped and cheered. The walking computer, which came out of nowhere said, "You have done well. You have saved us from the evil forces. What would you like as your reward A.D?"
"I want to go home," said A.D "But I promise I'll come back and save your world again if you need me to."
"Take this," said the walking computer. "It's the latest phone. You can call from it in any time zone. Hop into the tube."

So Sam got into the tube and found himself at home. He looked outside the door, where the school bus was waiting for him. Before he ran to the bus, he found a little white bird. It was a dove. There was a rope tied to it. Then our hero, Sam, knew just what had made him A.D, the hope for the human race.

By James, aged 10
Longford CE Primary School

 AWARDS FOR IMPROVEMENT JOINT WINNER

JOURNALISM

Lizo Mzimba wrote...

The key thing to remember when you're writing a report is to get the right information across. That means telling people what's happened, who it happened to, where, why and how.

You want to keep people watching or reading so, at the start of your report, try to get across the excitement or importance of what happened. This will make sure that the story really comes alive.

If you're writing a TV script, the vital thing is to make sure that the information is very clear and tells the story in a very straightforward way. This is something we always try to do on reports for *Newsround* because, when you listen to a TV report, you only get one chance to understand it.

If you're writing for a newspaper then you can afford to be more detailed. But you should still try to make sure it's not just dull description. Remember that your headline should, in just a few words, make someone want to find out more.

So take a good look at the picture you've chosen, decide what you think is happening in it, and then write your story in a way that makes the person listening or reading feel as though they were actually there.

Children were asked, in groups, to choose one of these
pictures and to write a newspaper or TV report about it.

INTRODUCING THE JOURNALISM

Lizo Mzimba's advice on writing a TV or newspaper report was taken to heart by our winners, who used the three stimulus pictures in very imaginative and varied ways. The results are engaging and topical, with some catchy headlines!

The budding journalists of **Knowle C of E Primary School** amusingly describe an incident at a local football match – it's not every day a hot air balloon lands on the pitch in the middle of a game.

The headline of the report from **Mary Exton JMI School** – *Super Sherbet Sails the Skies!* – would certainly catch the reader's eye, and keep your attention right to the end.

The interviews in *Flood Disaster on the South Coast* from **Croft C of E Primary School**, and *Disaster Strikes – Devon's Drowning!* from **St Cuthbert's RC Primary School**, really bring the situations to life. The interviews are very varied – lifeboat crews, the public, a meteorologist – and seem totally realistic. Even without a TV picture, the clear writing makes it easy to understand exactly what happened.

The well-crafted story, *American Star Fighter Plane Falls Out Of The Sky*, from **Selwyn Primary School** covers a tragic event in a realistic yet sympathetic way. You can almost imagine readers writing in to offer help to unlucky Saranjeet.

Elleray Preparatory School's amusing piece, *The Mayor Takes An Early Bath*, is a fantasy account of a UFO landing. The involvement of the army and the police in the report add a sense of realism, balanced nicely by the humorous comments from the local mayor.

The highly descriptive account of a bombing incident from **Glebelands Primary School** – *Morris Seeks Revenge* – combines serious and comical elements into an enjoyable and well-paced story.

Spinfield Combined School's *Daring Daniel Makes A Riverside Rescue!* uses a mixture of hard facts and human interest to make an engaging article, including a vivid interview with Daniel, the hero of the flood disaster. The residents of Sion also suffered flooding, as described dramatically in **Dorchester Middle School's** report, *Showers Submerge Sion*. This moving piece grips the reader with its account of the power and devastation of torrential rain.

Footie Surprise!

Liverpool and Birmingham had the shock of their lives on the 16th April, when Mr and Mrs Sparks landed on the pitch in their hot air balloon.

Liverpool were about to take a penalty when the hot air balloon landed and the ball shot into the basket.

The man (aged 38) and the woman (aged 36) were very embarrassed. Mr Sparks said, "I am extremely sorry but I ran out of gas to keep me up in the air!"

The match has been reset to Sunday 30th April. This is a relief to Birmingham City as the penalty to Liverpool doesn't count.

Here is Ian Bennet to say how he felt when it happened.

"I was very shocked when I saw it and I was amazed that nobody realised it."

Here is a Blues supporter called Phil Carter who was at the match.

"As I was very stressed that L'pool were going to score, when the hot air balloon suddenly landed, I was stunned."

The reason for Mr & Mrs Sparks being in the hot air balloon was that it was Mrs Sparks' birthday.

So happy birthday to Mrs Sparks who has recently turned 36.

By Victoria Cotter-Wall, Katherine Gough and Emily King, aged 10
Knowle C of E Primary School

WEST MIDLANDS WINNERS

Super Sherbet Sails the Skies!

On the 9th April, Sherbet the puppy caused a sensation when he won the national hot air balloon race at Pinehill playing fields.

Sherbet the 10-month-old Labrador was playing with his bone. While his owner's back was turned, Sherbet tossed his bone a little too high and it got stuck in the burner pull.

The puppy managed to take off and stay in the air because, every time he jumped to retrieve his bone, he activated the burner. As his flight continued he was seen by the other competitors. We asked one of them what he saw. "All I could see was what I thought was an empty balloon, nobody realised that there was a dog inside!"

"It must have been at least half an hour before anyone realised there was a dog on board!" said another competitor.

By now the competitors were so fascinated by Sherbet that they lost interest in the race and began to follow him. Eventually, Sherbet got his bone from the burner pull only to get it caught in the release vent.

That caused the balloon to deflate. The balloon gradually sank down in a nearby school field where the football team was in the middle of a game. Fortunately nobody was injured, including Sherbet, as the balloon canvas had been caught on a boundary tree causing Sherbet to topple out.

We asked one of the players what he thought of the event and he told us that he and his friends were left speechless.

When Sherbet was reunited with his owner, he laughed as he said, "I'm overjoyed to get him back, but I'm glad he isn't human otherwise we'd be paying for the repairs."

By Lucy Franklin, Emily Thomson, Louise Chapman and Kathryn Thompson, aged 10
Mary Exton JMI School

 EAST OF ENGLAND WINNERS

Write Here, Write Now

Flood Disaster on the South Coast

Vicki: Hello and welcome to Newsround, with Vicki Baker in the studio with the latest news.

We have a disaster on the South Coast of England in Kent. The city of Gillingham has been flooded and the situation is critical. The rain has not stopped for the last two days, which has caused the River Medway to burst its banks. Lifeboats are attempting to evacuate the city as we speak. For most people there, this is a serious problem. Many people are desperate to save their lives. All electricity has been turned off for safety reasons. The banks of the River Medway have finally given way after ten years of withstanding the current.

But for one lucky family, the Robinsons, a rescue boat has already arrived as you will hear. Matt Holsten is live at the scene.

Matt: Thanks Vicki.

Many people have drowned as a result of this terrible disaster. Only a few people have survived after being immersed in the freezing cold water. As you can see the wreckage of houses is floating all over the city. Many flats and buildings have been destroyed. Lifeboats are still saving people all round the city. One lucky family, the Robinsons, have finally managed to escape from their house by using the bedroom window. After crawling through it they succeeded in climbing out of the house into a rescue boat. They were brought to safety but the house was destroyed, moments later. Now back to the studio.

100

Vicki: Thanks Matt for that story. Now we are going over to speak to Anthony, who is interviewing Michael Anderson, Captain of the lifeboat crew and responsible for organising the rescue of the Robinson family.

Anthony: Michael, how did you feel when you rescued the family?

Michael: I was a bit nervous but they were in danger and needed saving so I'm sure I did the right thing.

Anthony: Do you reckon anyone else is stranded out there?

Michael: Yes, there are probably quite a few people, but I'm sure many of them will be rescued by boat eventually. We would urge people not to attempt to swim as this may put their lives at extreme risk.

Anthony: Do you think you are putting your own life at risk?

Michael: I became a lifesaver because I wanted to save other people from serious accidents or situations such as this.

Anthony: Do you enjoy being a lifesaver?

Michael: Yes I do because although it's often dangerous I think it's very important that everyone is safe.

Anthony: How do you feel when you rescue people?

Michael: I feel happy saving people and glad that I've rescued them alive. I think my job is extremely important and I will carry on doing it.

Anthony: Thanks Michael, and now back to the studio – Vicki.

Vicki: Thanks Anthony. Now you're probably wondering how and why the River Medway didn't flood earlier. Well the river has been slowly eroding away its banks over the past decade, so it was certain that it was eventually going to flood. But although they knew this information, scientists have been astonished by the sudden collapse of the river banks. They thought that the banks should have lasted another five years and that it was extremely unusual for the river to flood so early. The scientists however were aware of the growing danger and had already organised the construction of small streamways to carry water from the Medway in times of heavy rain. Many people think that it was not natural causes but humans themselves, interfering with the water course, that caused the river to flood. Now we're going over to Isaac King who is interviewing Dermond Ruspark, a scientist from The Institute of River Erosion and Environment Control, in London.

Isaac: Dermond, do you believe that it is humans that have caused the floods?

Dermond: No, I think it was completely natural for the river to flood and the fact that people were working on it is completely irrelevant.

Isaac: Do you agree with the other scientists that the banks flooded earlier than expected?

Dermond: Yes I do, and I also think that it is extraordinary that the banks have given way so quickly.

Isaac: Thanks Dermond. Okay that's all from London so back to the studio.

Vicki: Thank you Isaac King for that report. Let's hope the flood waters in Gillingham stop rising as soon as possible.

Sorry, that is all we have time for, but we will be back with the latest news on the situation in Gillingham at half past five this evening. Goodbye.

By James Emmerson, Katie Wilson, Liam Jackson, aged 10, and Jack Caulton and Nick Barnard, aged 9
Croft C of E Primary School

YORKSHIRE AND HUMBERSIDE WINNERS

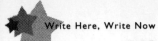

DISASTER STRIKES –
DEVON'S DROWNING!

Andrew: All coming up tonight –

This is Andrew McKay speaking. A disastrous flood strikes in the jolly village of Cotford St Luke. We find out the damage being done by the raging water. Over to Laura live in Devon.

Laura: Thank you Andrew. Here I am in Cotford St Luke where this dreadful disaster is happening. Fortunately I am high up on this hill, but when I look down on to the village it's a dreadful sight, people swimming for their lives in water 1.5 m deep. The fire brigade is still down there rescuing people. This flood has been going on for 24 hours but some floods have been known to last longer. I have a feeling that this one will be just the same. The people of the village say that the water levels have been building up for over a week. But they have only one question which I would also like to find out, where did all the rain come from? Perhaps Chloe can find that out as she interviews Dr Nelson, who is a meteorologist, later on in the programme. Or could this be anything to do with the day, Friday 13th? Now, over to Chloe.

Chloe: Thank you Laura. Here, we have Luke Elliff, a local fire brigade officer. So Luke, how are you handling the flood situation?

Luke: We have been up all night, saving lives. We have managed to save 30 lives so far. All the fire engines are out and there is no point sucking up the water because water keeps coming in. We're borrowing boats from the Sea Cadets for food and drink to be transported to Cornwall, where the people are going to be staying. Everything seems to be going fine at the moment.

Chloe: Thank you Luke. Now we go to interview a meteorologist. Here is Dr Nelson. He is going to tell us why this is happening. So, how come we get so much rain these days?

Dr Nelson: Well Chloe, it's actually to do with our jobs. The fumes that come from chemical factories are damaging the ozone layer and letting ultra-violet rays shine through. The chemicals in the air are causing acid rain.

Chloe: Is there anything we can do to stop this happening?

Dr Nelson: We would have to find re-usable energy. That is the only solution, unless, we scientists manage to find another solution.

Chloe: Thank you Dr Nelson. Now, over to Laura, who is going to interview Mrs Maginty.

Laura: Thank you Chloe. Now, I am going to interview Mrs Maginty, who is a victim of the flood. Hello Mrs Maginty. So, how do you feel about this awful flood happening?

Mrs Maginty: It has given me a great shock. I was in my lounge, nearly asleep, when I saw water trickling down the walls. Then, all of a sudden, a great wave of water came bursting through the wall. It washed me out of my house. I was so scared. The flood took me to the bottom of a hill. I climbed up to be safe and here I am.

Laura: I hear that you saved your cat's life, is this true and are you happy to have saved him?

Mrs Maginty: Yes, it is true. My dear Tibbles is lovely. I grabbed him by the tail as we were floating out of the house. I love Tibbles to bits. I'm so happy I saved him just in the nick of time.

Laura: Where are you going to live until the flood is cleared up and the rain stops?

Mrs Maginty: The fire brigade has found a house in Cornwall for me and the other people in the flood. It's cosy and warm. It's a bit of a squeeze with 30 people. It'll be our home until the flood is cleared.

Laura: Thank you Mrs Maginty. Now back to Andrew in the studio.

Andrew: Thank you to tonight's reporters and special guests. I am Andrew McKay in the studio for BBC News. The weather forecast is supposed to be rain all week which is a shame for Mrs Maginty and the other victims of the flood because the flood will probably continue. We'll bring you the latest update on the flood soon. Thank you for watching and goodnight.

By Chloe Robinson, Laura Hopper, Andrew McKay and Luke Elliff, aged 10
St Cuthbert's RC Primary School

 NORTH EAST WINNERS

107

AMERICAN STAR FIGHTER PLANE FALLS OUT OF THE SKY

Disaster struck the beautiful city of Amritsar in the Punjab last week when an EV-92 fighter plane appears to have fallen out of the sky and crashed onto a densely populated area of the city, killing over fifty people.

Among those still missing are the two crew members of the fighter plane. But amazingly, Peter Macpherson, the pilot of the sophisticated plane, survived the horrific accident.

When we questioned him yesterday he said, "I thought that we were safe in the EV-92. But now I know that there are obviously some problems which will have to be sorted out. This accident should never have happened."

Witnesses to the crash report seeing flames coming out of the clouds. Then the fighter plane appeared to just drop straight out of the sky, like a heavy stone.

In the enormous explosion which followed, those who weren't killed instantly were badly wounded by burning pieces of metal flying through

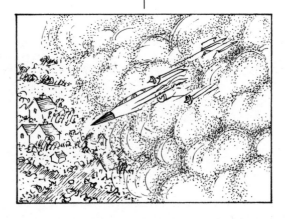

108

the air. The wreckage covered an area of over a kilometre.

Peter Macpherson will be interviewed by aircraft experts as soon as he is strong enough. They will want to find out how such a terrible disaster could have struck one of the most advanced aeroplanes in the world.

Rescue workers have not yet managed to locate the aircraft's black box, which could throw more light on the reason for the accident.

Rumours are beginning to circulate that sounds of shooting were heard immediately before the crash and that bullets were seen to be fired at the aircraft. The army is refusing to confirm that a terrorist attack might be responsible. They say that so far there is no real evidence to support this theory.

Other reports are being circulated that there is a serious design fault on the fighter plane and that the designers have been trying to cover this up for some time.

Peter Macpherson says, "I will certainly not be flying again until the EV-92 has undergone extensive tests."

All of these theories will bring little comfort to the family of Saranjeet Singh. Saranjeet lost not only his home, but also his grandparents, parents, brothers and sisters when the plane hit his house.

"My sister and I were just clearing away our dinner plates for our mum," reports Saranjeet, "when there was a massive explosion and everything went dark. The next thing I remember is waking up to find that I was lying in the road, surrounded by dust and bricks."

Saranjeet is now waiting for an operation to remove metal from his legs and hands. Doctors are afraid that he will never recover from the shock of losing his whole family in this awful accident.

By Sukhchain Bansal, Sami Ullah and Sagar Patel, aged 9
Selwyn Primary School

LONDON WINNERS
NATIONAL WINNERS

THE MAYOR TAKES AN EARLY BATH

A UFO landed in the middle of Lake Windermere causing a gigantic tidal wave, flash floods and a tornado at 8.00 this morning. The whole of the surrounding area was under water.

The Mayor, who had just arrived back from sunny Spain, was catching up on his work in his office at Hodge How. When asked how he felt the Mayor answered, "I am distraught. It is a dramatic change from sunny Spain to waterlogged Windermere."

Jill Dye, the owner of the local hairdressing salon Aqua, told us that all her hair products and computer were floating on the water. The customers who were having their hair coloured left the shop with multi-coloured dye running down their faces. Clients were floating out of the shop with their curlers in their hair and a dryer over them. Jill said angrily, "I'll get those aliens back, they have ruined my business. I am bankrupt."

After the effects of the devastation the fishermen of Windermere Anglers Association had a great time. All of the fish were biting.

The local schools were in chaos. The headmaster of Tree Top Primary School, Mr Pike, had offered to share the news. "It is a disgrace, the books have sunk to the bottom of the school. The chairs have floated half way down Lake Road. All the local anglers in full waders are trespassing in the school grounds. The pitch is a haven for fishing."

The UFO which had caused the tidal wave was bobbing into the bay by Cockshot Point. A hatch opened on the top of the ship and a little boy has been seen coming out. The boy was green and had blue hands. He walked down the side of the purple spaceship on his hands. Doctor Heart, who was taking his morning stroll when the boy came out of the hatch said, "I could not believe my eyes. I have never seen such a funny looking person in all my years as a doctor in Windermere."

It was also reported that a tall thin figure with four fingers on each hand had come out of the spaceship. He had greeny blue skin, big black eyes and was heard to be making loud clicking sounds.

The army and the local police are investigating. The Army Corporal, stationed at Liberty Lane Barracks, calmly told us not to worry. "We have full surveillance on the area. Although they are hostile do not panic. Do not approach them because they have been seen to have poisonous gas coming out of tubes, from their hands."

The Mayor was heard screaming, "I wish I had stayed in Spain!" as he disappeared down Troutbeck River with pikes snapping at his toes.

By Helena Jury, Jacob Jaeban, Storm Clarke Webster, Sophie Hicks, aged 10, and Joe Bolger, aged 9
Elleray Preparatory School

 **NORTH WEST WINNERS**

The Rising Sun

MORRIS SEEKS REVENGE

On Friday 13 June a devastating bomb blew up Sunrise School in Leicester. No one was hurt. Mr Duke, the head teacher, was horrified by this vicious attack on the school. We interviewed Mr Duke who was sobbing when he said, "Why did it have to happen to my school? Who could do such a despicable thing like this? To take away my hopes and dreams of directing another one of my brilliant key stage 2 musical productions with the children in this school. I am heart broken!" A man is currently being held in custody at Mount Leys police station, as he is the chief suspect.

At 6.42 pm a terrible rumbling quaking noise, which shook the house, disturbed Mrs Ashton of 817 Dreamday Crescent; she collected her children together and ran out of the house to investigate. As she stepped out of her front door she saw a thick black mushroom of smoke in the air above the school grounds. "It was terrifying, I had no idea what had happened, bits of debris were dropping all over my newly mown grass! My washing was really dirty and I had to do it all over again. I ran inside and rang the emergency services immediately. Then I jogged round the corner to find out more. I froze in horror, I could not believe my eyes, all I could see was smoke and rubble. Out of the corner of my eye I saw Mr Duke jumping madly waving his arms about shouting, 'Call the police!!!'"

Inspector Clevercloggs (Governor of the school) was the chief investigating officer. His team had discovered, after hours of sifting through the debris, that the bomb had been planted in a computer which had been donated by Mr Morris, head teacher of Weedstick School, almost exactly a year ago, as a present for coming first in the league tables last year. Inspector Clevercloggs gained a search warrant and went to search the home of Mr Morris. They discovered some interesting facts including conclusive evidence that Mr Morris intended to blow up Sunrise on this day. He was taken into custody and interviewed for further information. He confessed to Inspector Clevercloggs that he had planned this for some time.

I managed to get an interview with Mr Morris. I asked him, "Did you blow up the school?" He replied, "Yes I did, I planned it well over a year ago. I just had to be the top of the league tables. There was no other option but to blow them out of the charts. So when I was drinking a cup of tea one Sunday morning last year I had a moment of inspiration: wouldn't it be GREAT to donate a computer to Sunrise! Oh what a brilliant idea. I could so easily put a little old bomb in the back of the computer for when I really needed it. Such good planning. Well, when Sunrise won the league tables yet again, it was not good; I just had to blow the place to smithereens." He chuckled in a northern accent. "At lunchtime I secretly entered the computer suite and entered the code to activate the bomb, which was connected to my own home computer. I went home to prepare for my glorious moment. TOP OF THE LEAGUE TABLES AT LAST."

The cost of rebuilding the school will be in excess of £5,000,000, the National Lottery has kindly agreed to pay half, the local council have agreed to find £4,900,000 leaving a deficit of £100,000. The children are trying to help as much as they can by selling their toys, holding a fair, selling ruins of the school as souvenirs and charging for guided tours of the site. We eagerly await the completion of the new school.

By Sheena Kotadia, Thomas Newell, Grace Ablett and Callum King, aged 10
Glebelands Primary School

 EAST MIDLANDS WINNERS

WONDERS OF THE WORLD!

DARING DANIEL MAKES A RIVERSIDE RESCUE!
Brave neighbour hailed a hero!

Quick thinking 37-year-old Daniel Hockley was crowned King Lifesaver last night after courageously rescuing his neighbours from their flooded homes in the peaceful riverside village of Petersville, Cumbria. Daniel peered out of his window and was dumbstruck when he saw thousands of gallons of water rushing towards him down the street. Unknown to Daniel the ageing dam, ten miles down the river Sull, had burst!

As quick as lightning, Daniel leapt out of his bedroom window into the five-foot deep water below. Showing considerable bravery and courage, Daniel waded through the ice cold water and dragged his grandfather's sixty-year-old rowing boat out of his flooded garage and rapidly paddled out into his village, where he heard his neighbour Miss Laura Hay crying wildly to be set free. He struggled to climb up the

slippery drainpipe. Then with no explanation he grabbed his shaking neighbour, and keeping a firm hold of her arm he jumped out of the tiny window and almost breaking the old, shambled boat, he landed with a bump. After his phenomenal rescue Dauntless Daniel went on to save all his other twenty neighbours.

Very soon the atrocious flood will flow away and lives will be back to usual.

"I could only think of my stricken neighbours being trapped in their flooded homes. I thought I should at least attempt to save their lives!" said a breathless Daniel after his dramatic rescue.

"I was the last to be saved! I was crying with joy when I saw Daniel and the whole neighbourhood rowing towards me in that rickety old rowing boat."

"Daniel is a credit to the neighbourhood and is such a brave man!"

By Christina Pyke and Elise Spicer, aged 10
Spinfield Combined School

 SOUTH EAST WINNERS

SHOWERS SUBMERGE SION

The large lowland town of Sion is swimming this morning after torrential rain overnight. "This has been caused by too much rain on the mountains which has travelled down and flooded the river Deary, which runs through Sion," said the Mayor.

Sion Primary School struggled to evacuate after water had come crashing in through a classroom wall. No one was thought to have died, but 12 students and two teachers have been severely injured after the impact of water.

In the early hours of this morning the town and mountains of Sion were suddenly struck by torrential rain.

The town wasn't the only thing to be hit, farms around were hit too. Cows and sheep struggled to escape after water flooded their fields overnight. The water crashed through crops, and killed cattle.

We sent our reporter, Mac Bowley, to interview Mr George McKimber, a local farmer. "I was devastated but I didn't really have time to feel anything." This is disastrous for Sion and its tourist industry. It will be ages before Sion can restore peace to itself and its people.

This is Mac Bowley, Briony Gray and Katie Holmes saying goodnight to you!

By Briony Gray, Katie Holmes, Mac Bowley, aged 10
Dorchester Middle School